TO:

FROM:

A
BOOK
FOR
GRANNY

A
BOOK
FOR
GRANNY

BECAUSE
SHE KNOWS
BEST

LEE FABER

Michael O'Mara Books Limited

First published in Great Britain in 2011 by
Michael O'Mara Books Limited
9 Lion Yard
Tremadoc Road
London SW4 7NQ

Originally published in 2010 under the title *I Love You Granny*.

A CIP catalogue record for this book is available from the British
Library.

Papers used by Michael O'Mara Books Limited are natural, recyclable
products made from wood grown in sustainable forests. The
manufacturing processes conform to the environmental regulations of
the country of origin.

ISBN: 978-1-84317-666-4

1 3 5 7 9 10 8 6 4 2

www.mombooks.com

Designed and typeset by K DESIGN, Somerset

Printed and bound in Great Britain by Clays Ltd, St Ives plc

To my British grandchildren,

Kelly, Christopher and Sophie,

and to my American ones,

Austen and Jared.

I love you lots!

Contents

Being a good granny

There is a special bond between grandmothers and their children's children that seems to skip a generation. Grandmothers are always fun to spend time with because they are a storehouse of information, old-fashioned yarns and endless entertainment.

The best part is that a child of any age can get along with their grandmother and never have any generation-gap issues. Grandmothers have so much experience that they can tell at almost any time what the grandchild wants.

'It's such a grand thing to be the mother of a mother. That's why the world calls her grandmother.'

AUTHOR UNKNOWN

∽ **The first golden rule** ∾

You should hug your grandchildren as often as possible. After all, as American cartoonist Bil Keane once said: 'They invented hugs to let people know you love them without saying anything.'

'We need four hugs a day for survival.
We need eight hugs a day for maintenance.
We need twelve hugs a day for growth.'

VIRGINIA SATIR

∽ **What is a good granny?** ∾

The idea of a 'good granny' means different things to different people. There is no such thing as a perfect granny, just as there isn't a perfect parent. We simply have to do the best we can and learn from our mistakes.

A grandmother is …

❦ A mother with lots of experience.

❦ Old on the outside, but young on the inside.

❦ A babysitter who watches the kids instead of the telly.

❦ Short on criticism and long on love.

A child's perspective

One little girl, Sandra L. Doty, aged three and a half, put it very well when asked what a grandmother was. Her words were later reproduced on GranGran's This and That website. Sandra said:

> A grandmother is a lady who has no children of her own, so she likes other people's. Grandmas don't have to do anything except be there. If they take us for walks, they slow down past leaves and cater-pillars. They never, ever say, 'Hurry up.'
>
> Everybody should try to have a grandmother, especially if you don't have a television, because grandmas are the only grown-ups who have got time.

A good granny ...

- Listens to what children say ... and to what they don't say.

- Is somebody you want to visit ... to be with ...

- Will join Facebook so she can stay in touch with her grandchildren.

- May bake cookies, but won't let the children eat them between meals!

11

Granny and grandchild

When a grandchild is born it is like a miracle. The new grandchild is even more precious than one's own firstborn. The thing is, this love is usually returned 100 per cent.

'There is only one joy in life equal to the love of a child, and that is the love of a grandchild.'

JOHN MAJOR

✧ A special relationship ✧

Very little children generally see their grandparents as the provider of treats and pressies.

But as they get older, if you are lucky, your grandchildren may consider you to be a good friend; someone they can talk to about their hopes and fears. They may tell you things they wouldn't dream of telling their parents.

Parents versus grandparents

That difference is not because children think of their parents as ogres. But – as we all remember from our own experience of parenthood – Mummy and Daddy have a lot of pressures to cope with and very little time in which to do it.

If Grandma is simply there to listen, she will probably be rewarded with a close and enduring relationship with her grandchildren.

༄ Magic moments ༄

There are some special moments with your grand-children that simply catch at your heartstrings. These are things that grannies have to look forward to:

- When your grandchild takes your hand for the first time of their own volition.

- The first time they say, 'I love you, Granny.'

- When they ask for your advice.

- When they tell you their secrets.

- When they ask you if they can come to visit during half-term.

- When they tell you that you are the best cook/friend/ granny in the world.

❦   When they draw a picture just for you.

❦   When they send you a homemade thank-you note/
birthday card/Mother's Day card.

⧉ Love don't come easy ⧉

The catch is that you have to earn your grandchild's love.
And that doesn't mean showering them with presents or
being a mushy pushover every time they give you that heart-
stopping grin …

Here are a few pointers for building a strong,
nurturing relationship with your oh-so-special grandchild.

❦   Praise your grandchild for his or her achievements;
criticize their failures if you honestly believe they
could have done better. (Otherwise the praise means
nothing.)

❦   Be there (in spirit if not in body). Children need to feel
that someone is cheering for them.

❦   Don't compare your grandchildren with their parents,
their siblings or their other relatives. Every person is
different and abilities and personalities vary.

❦   Children will push you as far as they can. They need
limits and need to know you will stick to them. Be
strong and they will respect you.

W Make your home the welcoming sort of place that children want to visit. Nothing is worse than being dragged off somewhere they think is unpleasant or boring.

∽ When Granny goes too far ∾

Being a grandmother is truly wonderful – and every granny thinks her grandchildren are the best kids in the world. Sometimes, that overwhelming pleasure and pride *can* go to your head. Watch out for these warning signs, Granny!

'The idea that no one is perfect is a view most commonly held by people with no grandchildren.'

DOUG LARSON

You know you're an uber-proud granny when ...

W You change your name by deed poll to 'Granny'.

W You can't remember what colour walls you have – because they're covered, floor to ceiling, with your grandchild's artwork.

W You change your mobile ringtone to 'There's No One Quite Like Grandma' by St Winifred's School Choir.

- You find yourself wearing a fireman's hat/princess's crown/sheikh's turban at your local supermarket – because you were having so much fun playing with your grandchild you forgot to take it off when you nipped to the shops for milk.

- You write your occupation as 'grandmother' on official forms.

Proud grandmother

An elderly, wealthy woman in Florida was boring fellow beachcombers as she boasted on and on about her two remarkable grandchildren.

Unable to stand it any longer, one of her listeners interrupted her. 'Tell me,' she said, 'how old are your grandsons?'

Granny gave her a grateful smile and replied, 'The doctor is four and the lawyer is six.'

A visit to Grandma's

Nothing is more special than hosting your grandkids at your home. Whether they're coming round for a quick afternoon visit, staying overnight or for a week-long holiday, every moment – from the anticipation of their arrival to the bittersweet sadness of farewell – is there to be cherished.

Make every moment count.

'The handwriting on the wall means the grandchildren found the crayons.'

AUTHOR UNKNOWN

∾ Flying solo ∾

Whenever you look after your grandchild on your own, without their mother present, be mindful of the fact that it's as strange a situation for the child as it is for you, so be patient and be willing to compromise a little.

But don't panic! Remember, you are a mother as well as a grandmother and you can't have forgotten *everything* you knew about parenting.

TIP!

When your grandchild comes for a solo visit, never make the mistake of asking the child if they have had breakfast/ lunch/ dinner. The child will usually say 'no' and you will wonder why, before bustling around to remedy it.

Ask the parent instead and you may get a very different answer!

Common sense

The most important thing is to use your noggin. One new grandmother, in the process of feeding her infant grand-daughter for the first time, fretted over the fact that the level of milk formula in the bottle wasn't going down at all.

Having the sense to check the bottle, she discovered there was a cap between the milk and the teat so, of course, as much as the child sucked, nothing actually got into her. Granny quickly resolved the problem and feeding time resumed happily.

✿ The first visit ✿

The first visit should be short so that you can adjust to each other. Obviously an infant's needs are very basic compared with a toddler's. All you have to do is keep the baby fed, clean and dry.

If you are dealing with a toddler or an older child, you should have some activities in mind that you can do together. These are all good suggestions:

❧ Playing a game.

❧ Singing.

❧ Colouring pictures.

❧ Cutting out paper dolls.

❧ Reading to them.

Do your research

In advance, quiz the parents about what sort of things the child likes to do, play or eat. You don't have to reconstruct this, but it will give you a starting point.

Toy box

It's a really good idea to establish a big 'toy box' in your home, filled with age-appropriate toys: colouring books and crayons, puzzles, playing cards, picture books, and so forth.

19

This could be the time to get down from the loft all those toys you saved from your own children's childhoods!

Dressing-up box

As your grandkids get older, this is another excellent resource. Whenever you think of discarding something from your wardrobe – an old blouse, shirt, pair of shorts, scarf, belt, handkerchief, gloves or 'jewels' – put the item into a trunk, which will become the dressing-up box.

Make outrageous outfits from the clothes and stage an original play or cabaret, which you can write with your grandkids. Granddad and parents can be the audience.

Childproof your home

Having the grandkids to stay is an honour – but with it comes a bit of old-fashioned responsibility. A few tweaks to living spaces may be needed to ensure the kids will be super-safe in your house. Be especially careful in the kitchen, and think about installing a safety gate on staircases. Ensure all medicines and cleaning products are kept out of children's reach.

Sleepover sessions

O h, the excitement of your grandchild staying the night! Bathtime, tucking them in, bedtime stories … what pleasures there are in wishing them sweet dreams.

'When we were kids, grandmothers were old people. This is not just how we perceived them: old photos tell the same story. My grandma was very pretty and wore beautiful hats, but she was still old. Nowadays, grandmas are glamorous!'

PAT THORBURN

৩ Fun granny ৩

The success of overnight visits may depend on how much time you have previously spent with the child. If you are used to seeing each other on a regular basis, your house will be another 'home from home' for the child.

If distance separates you, you will have to make yourself fun to be with so that you never have to hear that dreaded, 'I want my mummy!'

The main thing to remember is that this is your glorious grandchild, whose parents thought you were competent enough to care for their precious child, so relax and enjoy it.

✍ Special traditions ✍

Routine can be a wonderful thing. There's something to be said for comforting familiarity and well-known (and well-loved) experiences. Why not fill your grandchild's stay with repeated joys and traditions that they'll experience every time? You'll be making the memories they'll remember childhood by.

'Perfect love sometimes does not come until the first grandchild.'

WELSH PROVERB

Stimulate their senses

We remember best through sensual experiences. Create some truly evocative memories by stimulating your grandchild's senses each time they come to visit. Here are some ideas:

- Touch – give them a well-worn teddy or a silky blankie to cuddle at night. Or perhaps they'll always touch the top of the wooden banister on the way up to bed.

- Smell – add a few drops of lavender oil to their pillow before they go to sleep.

- Sight – cover their bed in a colourful patchwork quilt. Make sure every bed they ever sleep in at your home is always made up with that same quilt.

- Taste – nothing tastes like Granny's home-cooked food. Serve it on a specially chosen plate for them that's their own for every visit.

- Hearing – sing them to sleep at night with their favourite soothing song.

∽ Bedtime ∾

One very important point is to make bedtime restful, rather than a battleground.

Make sure that supper is a pleasant interlude and that bathtime is a good experience. A bath toy will soothe a young child and divert their attention while you are washing their hair. Use no-tears shampoo and keep a little facecloth to hand – for holding over eyes while you are rinsing.

TIP

Girls with very long hair aren't much fun at bathtime, but you have to grin and bear it. Try very hard not to pull their hair as you tease out the tangles. A little conditioner in the rinse is a great boon.

Bedtime story

After they've brushed their teeth (supervised) is a good time for a bedtime story. Make sure you choose one that won't give them nightmares (although children can often have a different take to adults as to what is scary). See page 99 for some suggested titles.

Time for sleep

While official bedtimes can be bent a little bit, especially if your home is unfamiliar to your grandchild, you must be firm. Even infants can make you feel guilty by crying when you leave their room. Try not to be swayed, unless the child is very upset.

WHO WAS THAT?

After putting her grandchildren to bed, a grand-mother changed into old trousers and a shapeless jumper and proceeded to wash her hair.

She heard the children getting more and more boisterous until she finally thought, 'Enough is enough.' She wrapped a towel round her head and stormed into their bedroom, sternly telling them: 'Go to sleep!'

As she left the room, the three-year-old said with a trembling voice, 'Who was that?'

'If I had known how wonderful it was to have grandchildren, I would have had them first.'

LOIS WYSE

Breakfast with Grandma

The high spot of the sleepover could be breakfast the next morning. Usually anything children don't get to eat at home is considered a treat. Make yours a healthy one.

If you want to give your grandchildren a nutritious start to the day, forget sugary commercial cereals and make your own wholesome granola. You could even let the kids help you to make it. It will taste even better!

Homemade granola cereal

Makes about 20 servings

INGREDIENTS

    560g (20oz) porridge oats

    115g (4oz) wheatgerm

    55g (2oz) oat bran

    115g (4oz) brown sugar

    120ml (4fl oz) rapeseed oil

    115g (4oz) mild honey

    120ml (4fl oz) water

    1 tsp vanilla essence

    1 tsp ground cinnamon (optional)

    1 tsp salt

    170g (6oz) chopped dried fruit (dates, cranberries, cherries)

    115g (4oz) chopped pecans or almonds

    85g (3oz) flaked coconut (optional)

METHOD

1. Preheat the oven to 140°C (275°F/Gas Mark 1).

2. In a large bowl, mix together the porridge oats, wheatgerm and oat bran.

3. In a medium bowl, blend the brown sugar, rapeseed oil, honey and water. Stir in the vanilla essence, cinnamon (if using) and salt. Combine this mixture with the oats until evenly moistened, then transfer to a large shallow baking dish.

4.   Bake for 45 minutes in the preheated oven, stirring every 15 minutes, until lightly browned. Mix in the dried fruit, nuts and coconut (if using) and continue baking for 15 minutes.

5.   Remove from the oven. Allow to cool before storing in airtight containers.

'If becoming a grandmother was only a matter of choice, I should advise every one of you straight away to become one. There is no fun for old people like it!'

HANNAH WHITALL SMITH

Famous grandmas

Celebrity culture is a relatively recent phenomenon, but there have always been icons in the world of stage and screen. Some of our most beloved and accomplished actresses are now grannies in their personal lives.

Though it may seem hard to imagine these women burping a baby or tickling a toddler – accustomed as we are to seeing them in glorious haute couture gowns with diamonds glittering at their throats – these fine ladies have fully embraced grandmotherhood with relish.

'It's amazing how young grandmothers seem once you become one.'

AUTHOR UNKNOWN

৶ Julie Andrews ৶

Perhaps most famous for playing Mary Poppins in the eponymous movie, and Maria in *The Sound of Music*, Julie Andrews is a bona fide national treasure.

She has seven grandchildren in total. In *Parade* magazine, she spoke of her love of being a mother and grandmother, saying that these are the best roles she's ever had.

She also revealed that what she enjoys doing most with her grandkids is taking them into the garden and asking them how many colours they see, which makes them start observing.

Julie thinks being a grandma is wonderful because you get all the fun – but then every grandma knows that!

৶ Marlene Dietrich ৶

Usually described as 'glamorous', German-born screen legend Marlene Dietrich was certainly that. However, as famous as she was, she always insisted on having a private life, and in that life was a homebody.

In an anecdote published in *The Victoria Advocate*, playwright Moss Hart and his wife, Kitty, who were good personal friends of the actress, recalled once asking Marlene if she would stay for dinner at their New York penthouse apartment.

'Not a chance,' the actress had replied. 'Tonight I am having my grandchildren all to myself. Maria and Bill are going out and I am babysitting. You know, the one thing I can do is cook and Maria is letting me cook for the boys, give them their baths and put them to bed. I guess I'd rather do that than anything else in the world.'

๛ Vanessa Redgrave ๛

Vanessa Redgrave, an Oscar-, Tony- and Emmy-winning English actress, was born into a distinguished acting family and continued that dynasty when her own daughters Joely and Natasha Richardson followed her into acting. She has three grandsons and two granddaughters.

Vanessa laid bare her thoughts on grand-motherhood in this letter to 'her beloved Tash', written in 2007 and published in the *Daily Mail*:

> To be honest, I must confess that it wasn't until I became a grandmother ... that I realized just how important women are to children. Not just as mothers but as grandmothers, too ... Becoming a grandmother is the reason why women should make every effort to keep themselves as healthy as they can. [...]
>
> Like all grandmothers, I'm completely besotted by [my grandchildren]. They are all wonderful in every possible way.

✍ **Lauren Bacall** ✌

Who would have thought that Lauren Bacall – the mesmerising actress from films such as *The Big Sleep* and *To Have and Have Not* – was a twitterer? But she is – and several of her tweets are about her grandchildren (she has five).

In one batch of August 2009 tweets, she described a recent film viewing with her granddaughter:

> Yes, I saw *Twilight* – my granddaughter made me watch it, she said it was the greatest vampire film ever.
>
> After the 'film' was over, I wanted to smack her across her head with my shoe, but I do not want a book called *Grannie Dearest* written on me when I die. So instead I gave her a DVD of Murnau's 1922 masterpiece *Nosferatu* and told her, 'Now *that's* a vampire film!'

Fun with Granny

You don't have to resort to video games and TV to have fun with your grandchildren. Just remember the things you liked to do when you were a kid. It's quite probable your grandchildren will like them also, because they are enjoyable activities. Plus, they are spending time with you. Best of all, many of these activities are free!

'Being a grandmother is our last chance to act like a child without being accused of being in our second childhood.'

AUTHOR UNKNOWN

✆ Top activities ✆

The most popular activities grandmothers do with their grandkids are:

🌷 Going for walks (see page 110).

🌷 Going out for a meal.

🌷 Educational/cultural activities such as going to a museum (see page 108).

🌷 Cooking together (see page 86).

🌷 Playing games (see page 78).

✆ Outdoor activities ✆

These days, a lot of grandparents worry that their grandchildren aren't getting enough fresh air. These timeless pursuits are a great way to get them outside – and it'll be good for Granny too.

Fly a kite

Parks with large open areas free from trees, telegraph poles and electricity pylons are best for kite flying. Remember the fun you used to have?

Ride a bike

When was the last time you were on a bicycle? Never mind! You never forget how, even if you do wobble a bit at the beginning.

Get gardening

This is a fun and educational activity. If you have an allotment or garden in which you grow fruit and vegetables, let the children help you sow, weed and pick. This will give them an appreciation for food that beats plastic-wrapped edibles from the supermarket.

If you live in a flat, your options are more limited. But many types of fruit, vegetables and herbs can be grown either in window boxes or pots.

Play ball

There are dozens of games you can play with a ball. If you can't recall the exact rules of the games you liked when you were a child, don't worry. You could always make up a new game.

Camp out in the garden

Choose a day that is not too hot or cold. Put up your tent or rig something up with poles and blankets. Why not make up a flask of hot chocolate for the kids to add to the outdoorsy feel? If you have a campfire, you could even toast marshmallows or grill sausages!

✍ Indoor activities ✍

Sometimes weather, illness or home comforts keep you indoors with the grandkids. Happily, there's plenty of fun to be had here too ...

Record your own radio show

Set up the kids with a tape recorder and some interesting sound effects: dried beans in a can, a party blower, a whoopee cushion. Ask them to record a radio programme for you – or you could even co-host with them.

Don't forget to include adverts, play songs and have regular news reports.

Have a tea party

You can either use your own china (if you're not too worried about breaking something) or a child's tea set. Invite favourite teddies and dolls to be guests.

Use herbal tea (because it doesn't contain caffeine) in fruit flavours (because it tastes good). Add a little sugar and make sure it's not too hot for little mouths to drink. Serve with a plate of tiny sandwiches and mini cupcakes.

Why not get the dressing-up box out too? Fling on a string of pearls and act like you're all at The Ritz Hotel in London!

Play let's pretend

Another activity that could make use of the dressing-up box – or simply a game on its own; it can be played with or without props.

The children decide what the theme is and who will play each role – which does not preclude being animals, superpowers or mythical creatures.

Do a jigsaw puzzle

Keep a jigsaw puzzle set up on a table that you will be using for solely that purpose. Start with good-sized pieces that have different shapes and when the child has mastered these, graduate to more and more difficult puzzles.

Doing a jigsaw requires an awareness of shapes and positioning, which becomes important as children learn to read. Offer a little help, but try to allow the child to work out what goes where.

Have a sing-along around the piano

How about a few renditions of these traditional children's songs?

- 'There Was an Old Lady Who Swallowed a Fly'
- 'Row, Row, Row Your Boat'
- 'Ten Green Bottles'
- 'Old Macdonald Had a Farm'
- 'The Sun Has Got His Hat On'

Get googling, Granny

Modern technology – whether you currently think so or not – is actually a great boon to grannies. It's especially helpful for those whose grandchildren don't live near to them, facilitating frequent contact with an ease that would be unimaginable just decades ago.

So what are you waiting for? Hop on the Internet, turn on your iPhone and get to it!

'A mother becomes a true grandmother the day she stops noticing the terrible things her children do because she is so enchanted with the wonderful things her grandchildren do.'

LOIS WYSE

❧ Keeping in touch ❧

Not too many generations ago, families all lived together in the same village, town or city – grandparents, parents, siblings, aunts, uncles, cousins, nephews and nieces … Some families still do, but nowadays, work can often cast people out into far-flung places.

If the grandparents live on one side of the world and their offspring and grandchildren on the other, maintaining a close relationship can be difficult.

Tricks and tips

Here are some lovely ideas to help long-distance grannies keep in contact with their grandchildren:

🌷 Ensure that you touch base with each grandchild once a month on the date they were born – with a phone call, text message, email or e-card.

🌷 Send photos of each other back and forth via mobile phones or as email attachments. This will remind your grandchildren what you look like and keep you posted on their fast-changing looks (obviously, you'll need to get the child's parents to help with this at their end if your grandchildren are very young).

🌷 Declare the first day of every month 'Grand Day': get in touch by whatever means and ensure you have some contact with your grandchildren on this day.

- Get a jigsaw made of a photo of you and your grandchild and send them the puzzle piece by piece, so that they can put it together.

- Read a bedtime story to them over the phone. Make sure they have their own copy of the book you're reading, so they can look at the pictures.

Savvy solutions

Long-distance grannies everywhere should say, 'Thank goodness for technology!'

For even if you can't always get together with your family face to face, a computer, a mobile phone, a webcam and a free downloadable programme will keep you all in touch. Here's how:

- Mobile telephones can be used to text family when the cost of a call is prohibitive.

- Many mobiles these days have the facility to make short video recordings: perfect for parents to capture grandkids opening presents or the first bike ride.

- Email is a godsend and is sometimes preferable to texting, especially if the message you want to send is lengthy, or if you want to attach photos.

- If your grandchildren have joined Facebook and Twitter, perhaps you should sign up too. It'll be easier than ever to keep up-to-date with their lives.

❦   A little webcam and Skype on both ends allows you to talk in real time and see the person you are talking to.

TIP

For the uninitiated, Skype allows you to make free calls over the Internet to other people who have Skype software (which is free to download). Check out www.skype.com.

↬ A helping hand ↫

If modern technology has passed you by, don't worry. Grandparents are often impressed by their grand-children's skills and abilities in this area. After all, kids are usually ahead of their parents and grandparents when it comes to knowing the ins and outs of the newest gadgets. So ask them to set you up online.

If your grandchildren are too far away to teach you how to communicate with them via any of the above methods, ask the grandchild of a friend, who will often be happy to oblige.

In good company

You wouldn't be the only granny to ask for a little assistance. Probably the most famous grandma in the world, Queen Elizabeth II, was taught how to text by her grandchildren, Princes William and Harry. Now, she often uses her mobile to communicate with the princes and her other grandkids.

'If nothing is going well, call your grandmother.'

ITALIAN PROVERB

A right royal to-do

The Queen's learning process wasn't entirely straight-forward, though. She also asked the young men to help her set up her voicemail – with hilarious consequences.

For the high-spirited young royals decided to have a little fun with the message. When callers reached Her Majesty, they heard the following: 'This is Liz. Sorry I'm away from the throne. For a hotline to Philip, press one. For Charles, press two. And for the corgis, press three.'

DID YOU KNOW?

It has been proved that using the Internet can boost the brain activity of the elderly, slowing down or even reversing age-related loss of memory.

Californian scientists have found that the Internet stimulates the mind more strongly than reading and that the effects last long after the Internet session has ended.

✆ Internet experts ✆

Some grannies have truly embraced technology. Be inspired by the following enthusiasts.

The WikiHow wizard

Great-grandmother Sondra Crane, aged seventy-six, is the world's most prolific contributor to WikiHow, the online DIY manual about virtually everything.

She spends ten to twelve hours a day on her computer – researching, writing and exchanging ideas.

The social networker

At 104, Ivy Bean is not only the oldest person in Bradford, England, she's also the oldest Facebook member (with 5,000 friends), and the oldest devotee of Twitter. She has some 48,000 followers, who rely on her to explain the pros and cons of television programmes and to reveal old-fashioned recipes.

The blogger

Ruth1898, aged 109, was the world's oldest blogger. Inspired by the thought of passing along some of her many years of wisdom, she filed dozens of video blogs on www.growingbolder.com.

Memories to cherish

One of the most amazing things about being a grandma is the link you provide to your ancestors. You can remember your own grandparents, and can personally describe their lives to your grandchildren. Incredibly, five generations of family experience are shared between you.

'What a wonderful contribution our grandmothers can make if they will share some of the rich experiences and their testimonies with their children and grandchildren.'

VAUGHN J. FEATHERSTONE

✍ Simply priceless ✍

Don't underestimate the value of your memories, and those you can give to your grandchildren. After all, your grandkids will grow up in a very different world to the one you have known; in turn, their grandchildren will experience something completely different again.

It's important not to let memories and traditions die out. Record them for one and all to share in the years to come.

'In my granny's era, no one had a birth certificate. Birth dates were recorded in the family Bible.'

SUSAN DE ROBLES

✍ How times have changed ✍

In the writing of this book, many grannies contributed their thoughts on grandmotherhood, and also on how the world has changed since they were little girls.

Their stories make for remarkable reading, and just a few are recorded here for posterity, dotted here and there throughout this section.

⸺ Elaine McCalley (91) ⸺

My early childhood was spent on a ranch in the western US. We had no running water, no indoor toilet (though we had an outhouse), no electricity and, at that time, no telephone.

I remember going barefoot in the summer and swimming in the small local river. The winters were cold with lots of snow – long winter underwear was a pain, but necessary to keep legs warm. For the first three years of school, I went there in a covered wagon drawn by horses.

I remember Christmas trees were decorated with homemade ornaments and candle holders holding real candles, which my father would light for only a short period of time so as not to cause a fire. Oranges were a favourite stocking stuffer, as they weren't readily available like today.

⸺ When I was a girl ... (I) ⸺

When your grandchild asks you, 'What was it like when you were a girl, Granny?' the only possible answer is: 'Very different ...'

- We walked home from school, by ourselves, in any weather.

- We ate what was put in front of us.

- Tights didn't exist. One wore stockings attached with a garter belt.

- During school holidays, our mothers never saw hide nor hair of us from after breakfast until supper time.

- No one went to gyms to stay in shape (they either did a lot of manual labour, or a lot of walking or cycling).

- Hardly anyone was fat!

Our mums cleaned our faces with a handkerchief and spit.

'They say genes skip generations. Maybe that's why grandparents find their grandchildren so likeable.'

JOAN MCINTOSH

Granny's adventures

A grandmother was telling her little granddaughter what her own childhood was like: 'We used to skate outside on a pond. I had a swing made from a tyre; it hung from a tree in our garden. We rode our pony. We picked wild blackberries in the woods ...'

The little girl, quite taken with all of this, said, 'I sure wish I'd got to know you sooner!'

∽ Gillian Dallas (78) ∾

As a child, I loved playing in the garden. During the holidays, when my older brother Michael was home from boarding school, he invented exciting games for us to play. He was always the hero and I the maiden in distress.

After tea, Mummy would join us in the day nursery. All the toys would come out, a favourite being a swing, which hung from two big hooks in the lintel over the door. Then bath and bed. We slept in the night nursery at the top of the house. If Daddy was home in time, he would come and read us a story.

My favourite night was Saturday. Our parents would come upstairs to say goodnight looking so beautiful. I remember one particular dress Mummy wore – cream moiré silk, trimmed at the neck and cuffs with red fox fur. She smelt wonderful. Daddy looked magnificent in his dinner jacket, white silk scarf and opera hat. For our benefit he would tap it on his knee: it would come to life like a jack-in-the-box.

'I never flew in an airplane until I was fourteen, my mother never flew in an airplane until she was sixty-two, and my grandmother never flew in an airplane.'

SUSAN DE ROBLES

✒ Make a memory book ✒

Your grandchildren are probably much more interested in your own past (and in days gone by in general) than you might think. You may find that they love looking at your old photos and asking you what life was like in 'ancient times'.

Help them to appreciate your shared family history by making a personalized memory book that they will want to keep for the rest of their lives.

Which format?

You can either make your book the traditional way – using a scrapbook, photo album or notebook – or design it on the computer (which will allow you to print out copies for all the grandkids).

Or why not check out the website www.glorious grandchildren.co.uk? Here, you can create your memory book online – thus being able to share it instantly with all your grandchildren, no matter where in the world they might live.

Say cheese

Your memory book should contain as many photographs as possible.

Remember to label pictures clearly with the persons present and their familial relationship, the place and event shown, and the date it was taken. Who people are and what the photo is of might seem obvious to all concerned now, but decades from now those captions will come in very handy to your descendants!

TIP

Photos taken before digital cameras came into being can be scanned in order to create a digital file for use on a computer.

How to start

To give you some ideas about what to start writing about, you could begin with yourself and your own life, and then branch out into other memories you have. Don't worry too much about trying to do this in sequence. You can always fine-tune it later.

The most important thing is to have a record of what you consider to be significant. And don't self-edit: the trivial, day-to-day experiences are often those of most value to children. Why not ask them for advice if you're not sure whether to include something or not? They'll love to play a part.

What to include

Here are some starting points to get you thinking and writing. What can you remember?

You as a child

❧ When and where you were born

❧ Places and homes you lived in

❧ Your sisters and brothers

❧ Your mother and father

❧ Your grandparents

❧ Other relatives

❧ Your family life

❧ What your school life was like (achievements, report cards, the classroom)

❧ What you did after school, at weekends and in the school holidays

❧ Your friends

❧ Your special interests (sports, musical instruments, ballet, etc.)

Teenage memories

❧ Music you listened to and danced to

❧ Your first boyfriend

❧ The fashions you grew up with

❧ Newsworthy events

'If you want to civilize a man, begin with his grandmother.'

VICTOR HUGO

You as a young adult

- Scholastic qualifications

- What you did after you left school (travel, your job experiences)

- Your hobbies and interests (favourite books, films, music)

- Your first car

- When and how you met your husband/partner

- Your wedding and honeymoon

- Your children growing up

From then to now

- When and how your grandchildren's parents met

- Your grandchildren's births

- Your life since you became a grandparent

- People who have had a special impact on your life

🌷 What you wish for the future for your children and grandchildren

The world around you

🌷 How the world has changed since you were born, e.g. technology (TV, computers, the Internet, digital cameras), politics (Prime Ministers and other countries' leaders), the Royal Family, etc.

🌷 Where you were when world-shaking events happened (such as wars being declared, assassinations attempted, space flight realized) and your reactions to them

Family traditions

🌷 Christmas and other family celebrations

🌷 Birthdays and parties

🌷 Family recipes

Make it count

Record these memories how you wish – in a Q-and-A format, as a diary entry, in note form, as a letter to your grandchildren, in a book that charts your experiences year by year …

Your grandchildren will love looking through your memory book and asking you questions to learn more.

✤ Jennifer Poole (78) ✤

My granny lived in a very small flintstone cottage with only two bedrooms and no bathroom. She had an outside toilet, and her washing was done in a brick-built copper with a fire under it, which she had to get up to light at 6 a.m. It was only after the Second World War that she had her old stove taken out: it was replaced by an electric cooker.

Now a granny myself, I have watched my grand-children grow up in a completely different world – with microwave ovens, showers in the bathroom, washing machines, computers, and so on.

When they were small children, I watched as their schooling became very different to mine. I had to write with a pen with a metal nib in it and learn the three Rs, which included mental arithmetic, English grammar, geography of the world as a whole, and historical dates.

We had outside toilets in the playground. Senior girls served school dinners to the other children, while special meals were taken to the staff in the staffroom.

✤ When I was a girl … (II) ✤

- No one had a peanut allergy or an intolerance to wheat or dairy.

- All girls were taught to cook, sew and type in school.

- We hated going to the dentist – because if we had a cavity, the affected tooth was drilled without anaesthesia.

53

No one was ever 'on a diet'.

 We dressed up for dinner – always in black patent shoes and white gloves – and every Sunday for church.

 Only sailors and such had tattoos!

> 'Even the devil's grandmother was a nice girl when she was young.'
>
> GERMAN PROVERB

⮜ Susan de Robles (64) ⮞

When I was growing up, the evening meal was a family affair with everyone eating together. There were no such things as 'ready meals' or 'fast food'.

We called every adult Miss or Mrs or Mr as a sign of respect. We never used their Christian names. I don't think we even *knew* their Christian names!

My parents' word was law. 'Because I say so' was accepted as a reason.

We weren't allowed to pierce our ears until a certain age. Some of our mothers didn't have pierced ears. We weren't allowed to wear lipstick until we were sixteen. We weren't allowed to shave our legs or dye our hair either.

My father had a job; my mother's job was bringing up the family.

Wonderful wit

Every granny knows that her grandchildren are – among many other things – the wittiest creatures on earth. Admittedly, sometimes that wit is (ha ha!) unwittingly delivered.

Children can provide all sorts of humour in a granny's life – all of which simply adds to the pleasure of grandmotherhood.

'A friend of mine was asked how she liked having her first great-grandchild. "It was wonderful," she replied, "until I suddenly realized that I was the mother of a grandfather!"'

ROBERT L. RICE

Children say the funniest things

Children really do see the world from a completely different perspective to adults. Sometimes what they say is hilariously funny. Other times it is quite shocking. But often it is remembered and repeated *ad infinitum* by the grandparents …

Unstoppable

Granny was taking a walk with her grandkids in some of Cornwall's nastiest, windiest, wettest weather. The younger grandson never stopped moaning.

But the six-year-old battled on in silence, head down into the westerly gale. He said to his granny, 'I am going to get there. This is my Everest!'

Birthday

One four-year-old boy named Oscar asked his dad about being born.

His father told him he was born in the hospital on 16 December, to which Oscar replied with surprise: 'That's funny! That's the same day as my birthday!'

Who's boss?

One day, Katie was visiting her granny with her mother. As the afternoon unfolded, something came up in the conversation that her mum and granny disagreed about.

So Katie piped up to her mother: 'Granny is your mummy, isn't she?' Her mother concurred. 'Then you have to do what she tells you!'

Kissing the loo paper

A grandmother was in the bathroom putting on make-up under the watchful eye of her young granddaughter, as she had done many times before.

After she applied her lipstick, the little girl said, 'But Granny, you forgot to kiss the loo paper goodbye!'

Animal attraction

Midway through watching a nature programme on the telly, which showed reproduction in the ape world, Lee's eight-year-old granddaughter turned to her mother with horror and said, 'Mummy! Do you and Daddy do *that*?'

Rainbow

Gillian and her grandsons were out for a walk after a downpour one day, the children in their wellies, splashing through the puddles. They noticed one with a patch of oil floating on the surface.

Adam, the four-year-old, cried out, 'Look, Granny! There is a fallen rainbow!'

Retirement home

A teacher asked her young pupils to pen an essay on how they spent their vacation. One child wrote the following:

> We always used to spend the holidays with Grandma and Grandpa. They used to live here in a big brick house, but Grandpa got retarded and they moved to Florida, and now they live in a place with a lot of other retarded people.
>
> My grandma says Grandpa worked all his life to earn his retardment and says I should work hard so I can be retarded some day, too.

The pregnant fireman

'Give me a sentence about someone doing a good deed,' the teacher requested.

One boy raised his hand. 'The fireman came down the ladder pregnant,' he said.

The teacher asked, 'Sean, do you know what "pregnant" means?'

'Certainly,' the boy answered. 'It means carrying a child!'

Scientific silliness

Sixteen-year-olds in Arkansas, USA gave these answers to science exam questions ...

Q: Name the four seasons.
A: Salt, pepper, mustard and vinegar.

Q: What happens to your body as you age?
A: When you get old, so do your bowels and you get intercontinental.

Q: How can you delay milk turning sour?
A: Keep it in the cow.

Q: What is a fibula?
A: A small lie.

Q: What does varicose mean?
A: Nearby.

Q: What is a seizure?
A: A Roman emperor.

Q: What does the word benign mean?
A: Benign is what you will be after you be eight.

Holiday time

Holiday seasons are the times when families get together, be that to celebrate Christmas or to share a summer break. They provide the perfect opportunity for some extra special moments with Granny.

Holidays such as Christmas and Easter are inspirational for themed activities, while long hot days can be whiled away with plenty of fun pursuits outdoors.

Here are some lovely ideas for marking the holidays with your grandkids.

'A grandmother pretends she doesn't know who you are on Halloween.'

ERMA BOMBECK

✍ **Easter** ✍

A magical time for children (can you recall the excitement of all that chocolate?). Make it really memorable for them with these suggested activities.

Easter egg hunt

So fabulous it never falls out of fashion. Give each child a basket with a handle, lined with a fabric napkin, and have them search around the garden and/or your home for the chocolate eggs you've hidden.

You might have to help little ones find the booty: placing some small yellow chicks or colourful plastic eggs near the chocolate ones is a good idea.

Coconut cream chocolate Easter eggs

If you would like to make your own chocolate eggs, try this tasty recipe.

Makes 12 eggs

INGREDIENTS

    115g (4oz) butter, softened
    225g (8oz) cream cheese, softened
    900g (2lb) icing sugar, sifted
    ¼ tsp salt
    1½ tsp vanilla essence
    450g (1lb) flaked coconut

340g (12oz) plain chocolate

Icing, hundreds and thousands, or other cake
decorations to decorate (optional)

METHOD

1. In a large bowl, combine the butter and cream cheese.
    Add the icing sugar, salt and vanilla essence and mix
    thoroughly. Add the coconut and mix until well blended.

2. Put the bowl in the refrigerator to chill for at least one
    hour.

3. With clean hands, divide the mixture into 12 and
    mould into egg shapes. Put on a parchment-lined tray
    and refrigerate again for at least one hour.

4. Melt the chocolate in a microwave oven. Using a
    wooden cocktail stick, spear each egg shape and dip
    into the melted chocolate to coat. Arrange on a greased
    parchment-lined tray. If decorating the eggs, sprinkle
    with the decoration of your choice and allow the
    chocolate to harden.

5. Store in an airtight container in the refrigerator.

Egg heads

Have fun painting cold, hard-boiled eggs in this artistic activity
that's perfect for creative kids. Challenge them to paint
different characters on the plain eggshells: a businessman, a
glamorous lady, Humpty Dumpty, themselves ...

Just make sure you've fully boiled the eggs before you
start (otherwise the yolk will be on you!).

✎ Christmas ✎

Grandchildren at Christmas time are an absolute joy. Build their anticipation for the big day with these wonderful arts-and-crafts projects.

Paper snowflakes

YOU WILL NEED

- ❧ Sheets of white paper (any size, but try starting with A4)
- ❧ Scissors

METHOD

1. For each snowflake, fold one sheet of paper into quarters.
2. Using the scissors, cut out small shapes and designs from all around the edges.
3. When you unfold the paper, you will have a beautiful paper snowflake. And as in real life, all the snowflakes you make will be one of a kind!

TIP

You can paste your snowflakes on to coloured paper and use them for Christmas cards. Or why not try mounting them on a windowpane with two-sided Sellotape?

Christmas tree chains

You may find that you have to do the bulk of the work when it comes to creating these charming chains, as little fingers aren't always able to cut out such fiddly shapes.

However, even young grandchildren can colour in the trees once they're cut out, making this the perfect family project.

YOU WILL NEED

- A4 white paper
- Scissors
- Sellotape
- Pencil
- Coloured pencils and crayons
- Glitter
- Glue

METHOD

1. Fold the paper in half lengthways. Your paper will be approximately 10.5×29.5cm ($4\frac{1}{8}$ x $11\frac{3}{4}$ inches). Cut the paper along the fold.

2. You will now have two long strips. Put them together, one on top of the other, and fold in half horizontally, then fold again two more times. Open the paper up and tape the two short ends together securely, then fold into accordion pleats.

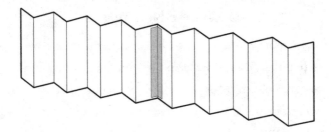

3. With the open edge of the paper to your right, pencil half a Christmas tree (split down the middle from top to bottom) on that side of the paper, with the branches going off the edge of the page. Cut out along the lines you've drawn.

4. Ensure that your grandchildren watch you open up the cut-outs. They will think it's magic! You will have eight joined trees when you open the paper up.

5. Now it's time to decorate the cut-outs. Colour in the branches and add baubles, fairy lights and other adornments. Why not use glitter and glue for the tinsel and the star atop the tree?

TIP

If desired, you can make paper doll chains using this same method. Simply draw half a boy or girl instead of half a tree, with the arms and legs going off the side of the paper.

∽ Chinese New Year ∾

This important event in the Chinese community is spreading in popularity and increasing its presence all around the world. The centuries-old festival is frequently celebrated with dragon dances – the ideal way for your grandkids to get involved.

Chinese dragon

Although this won't look as impressive as the huge dragons made for the formal celebrations, it's still a lot of fun to do!

YOU WILL NEED

- A plain white paper plate
- Pencil
- Scissors
- Coloured crayons
- Garden twine
- Swathes of lightweight, brightly coloured material – for example, sheets, tea towels or tablecloths

METHOD

1. Hold the plate lightly against your grandchild's face and mark with a pencil where the eyes, nose and mouth should be. Remove from their face and then cut two holes for the eyes, one for the nostrils to breathe and one for the mouth.

2. Give the mask to the child and suggest how they can decorate it with crayons to make a dragon face (adding scales, flaming tongues of fire, dramatic eyes and so on). If you really want to go to town, you could cut out individual scales from green paper and stick them on to the mask with glue.

3. Once decorated, cut two tiny holes on either side of the plate. Thread and knot two strands of twine through, in order to tie the mask to the child's head.

4. Drape their shoulders in the coloured material, perhaps tying it at their neck like a cloak.

5. Tell them to dance like a dragon, roaring all the while!

TIP

If you have several grandchildren, appoint one as the dragon's head and instruct the others to be the body. You will need lots more sheets, but they don't all have to be the same colour.

The children should dance one behind the other in a long line, twining in and out of furniture and grown-ups. Perhaps give the child on the end a feather duster to act as the dragon's tail!

∽ Summer ∾

The long hot days of summer are wonderfully glorious when spent with grandchildren. Make the most of the sunshine and try out a few of these ideas when the summer holidays come around.

Sandy skyscrapers

Children always love making sandcastles, so why not help them to construct something a little more ambitious when they're next digging in the sand? Here are a few ideas to get you started:

- Rowing boat
- Palace with moat
- Maze
- Racing car
- City skyline

If the kids are very young, build one of these exciting projects for them (keeping an eye out for little boys jumping on your prized creation – sometimes they'll destroy it faster than you can make it!).

Once it's finished, they'll spend hours playing with it … all thanks to Granny.

'Nobody can do for children what grandparents do.
Grandparents sort of sprinkle stardust over the lives of
little children.'

ALEX HALEY

Picnic pleasure

It's simply gorgeous to eat outdoors when the weather is
fine. Food tastes so much better! Put a rug in the garden
or go to a nearby park. Pack drinks and sandwiches, or for
something more substantial, homemade chicken nuggets
or fish fingers.

Fruit hedgehog

The perfect pudding for picnics, the fruit hedgehog is a
refreshing, healthy treat on any occasion. There's more than
one way to get your five-a-day!

YOU WILL NEED

- A large grapefruit
- A small orange
- Several different varieties of fresh fruit cubes
- Grapes, cherries and berries
- Further fruit and veg to decorate face
- A packet of wooden cocktail sticks

METHOD

1. Lay the orange and grapefuit on a plate with the orange in front. The latter will be the head of the hedgehog, the grapefruit its body.

2. Spear the fruit cubes, grapes, cherries and berries with the cocktail sticks and then skewer them all over the top and sides of the grapefruit.

3. Be creative as you decorate the orange. Make raisin eyes, cucumber ears and a carrot nose and … voilà! An edible hedgehog!

TIP

If you are travelling any distance, assemble the hedgehog on site. Pack the fruit separately in a plastic box and remember to take along the other bits and pieces you'll need.

Granny the carer

One role some grandmothers have always had is that of primary carer – actually bringing up the grand-children themselves. Statistics indicate that 200,000 grandparents in the UK are now sole carers.

In addition, some 70 per cent of families with babies and nearly half of those with toddlers rely on their grandparent carers. With lots of mothers now working part or full time to help pay off mortgages or maintain momentum in a career, grannies have become more involved in childcare than ever.

'Have children while your parents are still young enough to take care of them!'

RITA RUDNER

✎ What shall we do today, Granny? ✎

Regularly looking after your grandkids is an experience to cherish. You could make the most of the routine and book your grandchild a place on a weekly course in your area — maybe they could learn to swim or take up ballet while in your care.

✎ Education from an early age ✎

If your grandchildren have not yet started school — or even if they have — it's never too early or too late to start playing educational games with them at home. Developing skills that will help them in later life is to equip them with an advantage that will endure long after your afternoon sessions with them have ceased.

Kids these days can feel stressed about academic achievement, so never labour the point or put them under any pressure. You want your time with them to be fun. Happily, fun can still equate with learning with these cunning games and ideas.

Grocery store

Set up shop and take it in turns to play the cashier and the customer. Buy various objects and pay for them: this teaches children about making and using change.

This shopkeeping let's pretend game can also help improve maths proficiency, while familiarity in handling money is a real life skill to master.

'Some of the world's best educators are grandparents.'

CHARLES W. SHEDD

Spelling bee

Start with simple words, of course, but as your grand-children grow up, you can really challenge them with complicated words. Bring out their competitive spirit!

You can either ask them to spell words aloud, letter by letter, or to write them down in a spelling test.

Story time

Develop your grandchild's imagination by asking them first to tell you and later to write you stories. To inspire young kids, make up stories of your own to tell them – you may find they start arguing with you about what happened next!

Book club

For older children, add a comprehension element to their enjoyment of books. Ask them questions about the characters, the main themes, and how the story made them feel. Discuss the books in detail – just as you might in your own book club.

Where in the world?

Teaching your grandchild to be familiar with maps and globes is an excellent place to start when it comes to geography. Tempt their interest by describing different cultures and giving funny facts about time differences and changing seasons (for example, in Australia, they have barbecues on Christmas Day!).

If family live far afield, show your grandchild where they live on a map. At reunions, engage the child's imagination by asking family members to describe their unfamiliar homes to the child. A non-Londoner will be fascinated by stories of Buckingham Palace and bright red buses, while an urban child will adore hearing about cows and pigs.

Oldies but goodies

These traditional games never fall out of fashion. They've endured because they're fantastic fun to play – but they also come with some added educational benefits. For example:

- I spy – delights little children and teaches them the letters of the alphabet.

- Charades – unleashes the creative instincts in kids.

- Noughts and crosses – gives them a go at logical thinking.

- Pin the tail on the donkey – improves spacial awareness.

- Simon says – encourages children to listen closely to instructions.

Terrarium

A terrarium is a living landscape inside an enclosed container. It's a hands-on way of getting children interested in nature and biology. Making one with your grandchildren is a marvellous project indeed.

YOU WILL NEED

- A plastic or glass bowl, or other suitable see-through container
- Pebbles
- Compost
- Small rocks
- Branches
- Moss
- A variety of small plants
- Clingfilm

METHOD

1. To start, put a layer of pebbles on the bottom of your container for drainage. Cover with 5cm (2 inches) of compost.
2. Add a few pretty rocks, branches, moss and small plants. Water the plants, but don't soak them.
3. Cover the top with clingfilm. Water as needed from time to time.

TIP

If you are making this with a grandson, he will probably be delighted if you add some bugs or worms to the terrarium – but in this case, cover the top of the container with a fine wire mesh, cut to size, rather than clingfilm, so that the creatures have air to breathe.

❧ Famous grandparent carers ❧

Calling on the grandparents to help out with childcare is more common than ever. Naturally, grannies are always happy to lend a hand to assist busy mums, as these high-profile grans attest.

Marian Robinson

Here's to you, Mrs Robinson: the 'First Grandma'!

President Barack Obama's mother-in-law, Marian Robinson, has two children: First Lady Michelle Obama and a son, Craig Robinson. Mrs Robinson currently lives in the White House with her daughter, where she helps care for her two granddaughters: Malia, aged ten, and Sasha, eight.

Pauline Macaulay

The Ex-Prime Minister's mother-in-law came to the rescue when her daughter Sarah Brown had to travel to the US at short notice, in order to attend Senator Kennedy's memorial service as the UK's representative, in lieu of her husband, then PM Gordon Brown.

It was the first time that John, five, and Fraser, two, were on their own overnight with their granny. Sarah wrote out a list of favourite snacks and soft toys to accompany the boys ... before she realized that if anyone was up to the job, it was her mother.

Sarah says that mum Pauline has shown herself to be an expert at homemade chicken nuggets, snail-catching, junior gardening lessons and some very creative kitchen table projects!

Fun and games

This is the part most grandparents like best! Having the free time to play with the children is a special gift, and it's easy to see that kids really appreciate the many hours grandparents dedicate to having fun with them.

> 'My mother and stepfather are definitely from the new generation of grandparents; busy and active, learning new things and always volunteering to help others, but also making sure that they spend time with all their grandchildren.'
>
> SARAH BROWN

∞ What shall we play? ∞

To add a bit of variety to your time together, why not incorporate some of the following into your play sessions?

'Mairzy Doats'

For this old-fashioned but timeless game, you will need white paper and pencils, and either crayons or coloured pencils.

Its history begins back in 1944, when a very silly song entitled 'Mairzy Doats' hit the radio waves. It had a catchy tune and almost entirely senseless lyrics.

The song took playgroups and nursery schools by storm. Teachers played the tune on the record player and children drew loops on paper with a pencil in sync with the music. Then they coloured in the loops as garishly as possible. It was great fun.

'Mairzy Doats' today

If you can remember the tune, try it with your little ones. If you can't, make up or choose another one!

Board games

Every family has at least a couple of board games in the house. Young children can be taught how to play Snakes and Ladders, Chinese Chequers, Draughts, Cluedo, Monopoly or even junior editions of Scrabble.

Children love to play board games and some are educational as well as fun.

Smile

This really needs four or more people to be fun.

One person is selected to be 'it'. That person is the only one who is allowed to smile. The 'it' person has to do everything in their power to get the others to smile without touching them. The first person to smile becomes the next 'it'.

The winner of the game is the one who never smiles – which sounds rather glum, but is actually surprisingly difficult in this fun, contagious game.

Card games

Another enduring activity that can be enjoyed from a young age, this really gets the whole family involved. Here are some suggestions of games you could play – every family will have their own favourites!

- Go Fish

- Snap

- War (not as violent as it sounds!)

- Rummy

- Sevens

Grandmother's footsteps

One player is 'grandmother'. This player stands about 10 metres (25 feet) away from the other players, who stand in a straight line facing her. Grandmother turns her back on them.

The aim of the game is to touch grandmother on the back, without her seeing you move. All the players creep forward slowly, ready to freeze whenever grandmother turns around. Grandmother has to count to ten quietly before she can turn, but she can count as quickly or as slowly as she wishes.

When grandmother does turn, if she sees anyone moving, that person has to go back to the start. The winning player is the person who gets close enough to touch grandmother on the back without being spotted.

Outdoor games

Here are some all-generation outdoor games you might like to play with your grandkids:

- Croquet

- Rounders

- Kickabout (with a football)

- Tennis

Amazing grannies

Everyone thinks their granny is amazing in one way or another. But you'll no doubt agree that the following women's accomplishments put them some-where up in the stratosphere!

'My grandmother, she started walking five miles a day when she was sixty. She's ninety-seven today and we don't know where the hell she is.'

ELLEN DEGENERES

∞ The waterskier ∞

At ninety-four, Lucille Borgen became the oldest competitor ever in the US National Waterskiing Championships: the largest waterski tournament in the world. She amazed the crowd, winning the slalom and tricks title in her age division.

Lucille is an embodiment of triumphing over adversity. She survived polio as a child, cancer as an adult and the complete loss of vision in her left eye – but has never let anything stand in her way, winning more than 500 titles in her career.

✂ The holistic doctor ✂

Dr Gladys McGarey – the author of *The Physician Within You* and a doctor considered by many to be the mother of holistic medicine – was never going to let a little thing like age slow her down, even after passing the milestone of her eightieth birthday.

In 2005, at the age of eighty-four, Dr McGarey and her eighty-eight-year-old brother spent two months in Afghanistan on a medical mission, bringing health care to the neediest of people.

✂ The runner ✂

Rosie Swale-Pope, MBE, is a sixty-three-year-old grandmother from Tenby, Wales. She spent five years running 20,000 miles around the world to raise money for cancer charities, during which time she almost drowned in a river, suffered frostbite and double pneumonia, and was hit by a bus.

Her run took her through England, Holland, Germany, Poland, Lithuania, Latvia, Russia, the US, Canada, Greenland,

Iceland and the Faroe Islands. She covered every mile of land on foot, pulling her possessions behind her in a little cart.

∾ The shot-putter ∾

Ruth Frith, from Brisbane, broke a world record in the shot put at the age of 100. Her 4.07-metre throw on 11 October 2009 at the World Masters Games didn't just win her a gold medal, it also broke the world record.

She was the only competitor in the over-100s category, but Ruth never took anything for granted, training five days a week and regularly lifting 35kg (77lb) weights. The great-grandmother doesn't drink or smoke, but she doesn't eat vegetables either, claiming she hasn't liked them since she was young – don't tell that to the grandkids!

∾ The actress ∾

Mae Laborde, aged 101, is the oldest living Hollywood actress. Many people dream of being on the silver screen – Mae just hadn't realized her face would be so wrinkled by the time she finally made it in show business four years ago.

The Californian grandma is now sharing the screen with some of the biggest names in Hollywood. She has done TV adverts and shows, and even a feature film with Ben Stiller. 'I get some of the nice jobs,' she remarked.

৶ The political activist ৶

In January 1999, Doris 'Granny D' Haddock, a great-grandmother of sixteen, began a 3,200-mile walk across America to rally against big money in elections, walking ten miles each day for fourteen months. She was ninety years old.

She trekked through over 1,000 miles of desert, climbed the Appalachian Mountains in blizzard conditions and even skied 100 miles after a historic snowfall made roadside walking impossible.

Granny D celebrated her ninety-ninth birthday by lobbying for campaign finance reform at the New Hampshire State House.

Cooking with Granny

While some adults have mixed feelings about it, children love to cook. You may have fond memories of sitting perched on a stool, watching your gran rolling out dough, making cookies and cakes (and letting you lick the bowl).

Granny's kitchen was the room where love lived and you can create the same atmosphere for your grandkids by cooking and baking with them.

'If God had intended us to follow recipes,
He wouldn't have given us grandmothers.'

LINDA HENLEY

↩ Granny's little helpers ↪

Depending on the age of the child and your culinary ability, cooking and baking can go from simple to complicated. Young children are often happy to measure ingredients, stir, and taste-test the finished product, while older children and teenagers can usually participate in every step.

The main goal for cooking with children of any age should be fun, not perfection, so it doesn't matter if there are a few mistakes and a lot of mess!

TIP

Keeping a special apron for each grandchild will keep the mess off their clothes.

↩ A positive message ↪

Cookery sessions offer ideal opportunities to talk with your grandkids about the benefits of food as a fuel for energy and healthy growth. With growing numbers of young people suffering from eating disorders, food issues are clearly prevalent and a common concern for many.

Grandparents can help to develop healthy attitudes about food by talking about moderation, balance and the pleasures of eating well.

> ## TIP
>
> To reinforce this positive message, you might want to consider growing a small vegetable garden with your grandchildren. Kids are far more likely to enjoy vegetables if they have played a part in growing and preparing them.

✎ Cooking: the key benefits ✐

Kids benefit in a number of ways from participating in cookery sessions. Here are a few examples of the way a bit of baking can lead to more than just cookies …

Add up the advantages

Measuring ingredients and calculating changes to recipes to adjust serving sizes helps kids to make practical use of maths. Sometimes, even kids who struggle in school find that when they learn in a hands-on way, rather than from books, concepts that eluded them suddenly become clear.

Ask children to help with the mental arithmetic required and entrust them to measure items to the correct weight.

Travel the world

Cooking offers natural opportunities for learning about other countries and cultures. Grandparents can encourage children to try recipes that are native to faraway places, then both generations can research the country while sampling some of the nation's culinary offerings.

Share and share alike

Cooking for others develops skills that every child needs in order to grow up as a well-adjusted and polite member of society – the act of sharing, the art of consideration, the pleasures of hospitality.

Picture perfect

The favourite aspect of cooking for many children is the chance to decorate the end product – adding sugar pictures to cupcakes, generously sprinkling hundreds and thousands, adding silver balls to thick white icing, and (for the older children) practising their handwriting by piping icing through a nozzle.

All these efforts hone the kids' artistic skills and explore the idea of presentation.

✑ Granny's favourite recipes ✑

Baking with grandchildren is a joy like no other. The act of preparing food together satisfies a real nurturing instinct for Granny, while the kids love the fun and mess when they get involved. The tasty treats that follow are an added bonus!

Here are a few favourite recipes that will provide hours of culinary enjoyment.

TIP

Whenever children are helping out in the kitchen, grand-parents must always be on hand to supervise the use of sharp tools, electrical appliances and hot surfaces.

Additionally, children should be taught not to use kitchen chairs for climbing, instead asking for help to reach high cabinets or making use of kitchen steps. Safety first!

'Just about the time a woman thinks her work is done,
she becomes a grandmother.'

EDWARD H. DRESCHNACK

Crisp marshmallow bars

This is every small child's favourite treat. It's very quick and easy to make.

Makes about 32 bars

INGREDIENTS

45g (1½oz) butter or margarine

275g (10oz) marshmallows

170g (6oz) crisp rice cereal

METHOD

1. Melt the butter in a large saucepan over a low heat.

2. Add the marshmallows and stir with a wooden spoon until everything is melted.

3. Remove from the heat.

4. Add the rice cereal and stir until it is well coated.

5. Press the mixture evenly into a 33 × 22.5 × 5cm (13 × 9 × 2 inch) greased baking tin with a buttered spatula.

6. Allow to cool and then cut into 32 squares with a knife or pizza cutter.

Blueberry muffins

These tasty little buns are an idea stolen from America, where everyone has a favourite blueberry muffin recipe (or they cheat and use a pre-packaged mix).

This recipe produces a sweet, cake-like muffin that children adore.

Makes 18 muffins

INGREDIENTS

250g (9oz) fresh blueberries

2 tbsp plain flour

250g (9oz) plain flour

4 tsp baking powder

1 tsp salt

55g (2oz) butter or margarine at room temperature

340g (12oz) caster sugar

2 large eggs

1 tsp vanilla essence

240ml (8fl oz) milk

METHOD

1. Preheat the oven to 190°C (375°F/Gas Mark 5). Grease muffin tins or line with paper muffin cases.

2. Put the blueberries in a small bowl and sprinkle with the 2 tbsp of plain flour. Stir to coat the berries thoroughly.

3. In another bowl, stir together the remaining flour, baking powder and salt.

4. In a large bowl, whisk the butter or margarine with an electric whisk and gradually add the sugar. Whisk the eggs and stir into the creamed mixture along with the vanilla essence. Next, stir in the flour mixture alternately with the milk, mixing well after each addition. Finally, fold in the blueberries.

5. Fill the muffin cups three-quarters full with the batter and bake in the preheated oven for 25 minutes, until a cocktail stick inserted in the centre of a muffin comes out clean (except for the blueberries, which may be deceiving). Don't overbake.

6. Remove from the oven and cool on wire racks.

Granny's cookie pizza

This is a children's pizza, made with a chocolate-chip-cookie dough crust and a chocolate-and-peanut-butter topping. No wonder kids love it.

Some possible decorative toppings are suggested here, but let the children get creative!

TIP

Why not serve the cookie pizza in lieu of a birthday cake? It would certainly be different!

Makes one 37.5cm (15-inch) party-sized pizza

INGREDIENTS

Crust:

425g (15oz) plain flour

1½ tsp baking powder

1½ tsp bicarbonate of soda

¾ tsp salt

340g (12oz) caster sugar

170g (6oz) soft brown sugar

340g (12oz) butter

3 large eggs

1 tsp vanilla essence

340g (12oz) plain chocolate chips

Topping:

6 individual pots (62.5g/2½oz) chocolate mousse

250g (9oz) peanut butter

225g (8oz) vanilla yogurt

Plus decorations of your choice (sweeties, whipped cream, nuts, dried fruit, etc.)

METHOD

1. Preheat the oven to 180°C (350°F/Gas Mark 4).

2. In a medium bowl, mix together the flour, baking powder, bicarbonate of soda and salt until well combined.

3. Cream the two sugars and the butter together in a large bowl. Add the eggs and whisk until light and creamy. Stir in the vanilla essence. Add the flour mixture to the sugar mixture and whisk with an electric whisk until well blended. Fold in the chocolate chips.

4. Trace a 37.5cm (15-inch) circle onto a sheet of greaseproof paper. Press the dough into this and then transfer it, paper and all, to a baking sheet.

TIP

If you score the dough into wedges before you bake it, it will be easier to cut later.

5.   Bake for about 15–20 minutes, until it just begins to brown. Remove from the oven and set the pizza on a wire rack. Peel off the paper once cooled.

6.   Make the filling. In a bowl, whisk the chocolate mousse, peanut butter and yogurt together. Spread on the cooled cookie crust.

7.   Top in a decorative pattern with the treats of your choice: try whipped cream, chocolate chips, chopped chocolate toffee bars, Smarties, miniature marsh-mallows, chopped peanuts, dried fruit, fresh fruit or nuts.

8.   Cut with a very sharp knife into portions. If this fails, never mind. Just break off bits and enjoy!

TIP

This is also very, very nice topped with a scoop of ice cream.

Easy bread rolls

Lest you think we only ply our grandchildren with sweets, here's a recipe for some delicious savoury rolls.

Baking bread with children is an excellent way to ignite a passion for homemade food and to get them involved in the family catering; these rolls could be served with a wholesome soup at an informal family lunch. They're so easy to make, older kids could go home and dazzle their parents with their newfound culinary skills.

Besides which, of course, there's nothing more homely than the smell of baking bread…

Makes 12 rolls

INGREDIENTS

1 sachet (7g/¼oz) instant yeast

240ml (8fl oz) tepid water

1 large egg

55g (2oz) granulated sugar

1 tsp fine sea salt

4 tbsp vegetable oil

340g (12oz) strong white flour, sifted

butter to grease tins

METHOD

1. Dissolve the yeast in the tepid water.
2. Add the egg, sugar, salt and oil to the yeast and mix well.
3. Add half the flour and whisk until smooth. Add the rest of the flour and whisk again.
4. Grease a 12-cup muffin tin with butter. Fill each hole half full with batter, then cover with a tea towel and let rise until doubled in volume, about one hour.
5. Preheat the oven to 200°C (400°F/Gas Mark 6). Bake in the centre of the oven for about 15 minutes until golden brown.

'On the Mother's Day card we bought for Grandma, there was a picture of a glass half full of milk. The card read: "Some people look at this and think the glass is half empty, some people look at it and think the glass is half full. But a grandma sees it and asks, 'Would you like some cookies with that?'"'

AUTHOR UNKNOWN

Story time

There's nothing more comforting than snuggling down on the sofa with the children, plush cushions and a good book. It's great for both Grandma and the kids, promoting closeness and love.

This sort of setting associates reading with fun, not homework or a chore. You can instil the love of reading in your grandchildren: a passion that will last a lifetime.

'I was so flattered when Jago, who's nearly three, said he specifically wanted Granny to read him his bedtime story. As a result, I'm afraid I showed off and put on lots of funny voices.'

JILLY COOPER

✦ Anytime stories ✦

A child who enjoys a good book will do so throughout the day – not just at bedtime. Encourage reading as a daytime pursuit as well as a soothing night-time ritual. Both you and the child's parents will appreciate the quiet 'downtime' that follows.

Set aside a special story time when grandchildren come to visit you. After bathtime but before bedtime is a good time to wind down.

✦ Which books? ✦

Invest in award-winning and classic books for your grandparent library. Read the children's book reviews in the weekend newspapers for recommendations.

It's also a good idea to visit bookshops and actually look at the books. You will know after flicking through a few pages whether a book will be interesting.

Here are a few suggestions to start you off:

* *The Very Hungry Caterpillar* by Eric Carle

* *The Gruffalo* by Julia Donaldson

* *I Will Not Ever Never Eat a Tomato* by Lauren Child

* *Where the Wild Things Are* by Maurice Sendak

* *The BFG* by Roald Dahl

TIP

Little children like books with beautiful pictures. Older children can read to you from books you have chosen; these can be read a chapter at a time.

ೂ The gift of reading ೦

Give your grandchild a book for their birthday or Christmas to add to their own book collection.

Be sure to include a personal handwritten note to them on the inside front cover with the date and the occasion – it will mean a lot to them, both now and in the years to come.

ೂ The library ೦

Don't forget about this wonderful resource. Take your grandchild to your local library and teach them how to locate books by title, subject or author. You might even want to obtain a library card for them.

While you are there, you can enquire as to whether your branch hosts storytelling events – many do.

ೂ The spoken word ೦

Although the written word is a wonderful thing, it would be foolish to underestimate the power of storytelling as an audio experience. This is how children first come to stories, and is the soil in which their fertile imaginations grow.

THE WRITER

A little boy was pounding away on the keyboard of his grandmother's computer. He told her he was writing a story.

'What is it about?' she asked.

'I don't know, Granny,' her grandson replied. 'I can't read yet.'

Play the part

Really relish the act of reading aloud to your grandchildren. Put on silly voices and characterize the speech of different characters. Build tension by throwing in dramatic pauses at relevant moments and add flavour by introducing a scared or happy or angry tone to your voice as needed.

Your grandchild will be that much more involved in the tale you're telling, so don't be embarrassed!

Make up your own stories

Regardless of whether you consider yourself to be a good writer, there's nothing to stop you making up stories for your grandchildren off the top of your head and saying them aloud.

Invent your own protagonists, or place branded characters in imagined, personalized situations – Peppa Pig on holiday in Spain, for example (particularly good if your grandchild is on vacation in Spain or has just come back from there).

'Few things are more delightful than grandchildren
fighting over your lap.'

DOUG LARSON

Audiotapes

A rich resource of stories – but don't just leave it to the professionals. Why not record yourself reading classic tales aloud? Long-distance grannies could send the recording to grandchildren as another way of strengthening their bond.

Parents will probably be grateful for the in-car entertainment on long journeys, too!

✎ Stories beyond books ✎

It's a really great idea to encourage your grandchild's love of literature by including it in all aspects of their play. For example:

🌷 Let's pretend – your grandchild might love to play at being Noddy; guess that makes Granny Big Ears ...

🌷 Artwork – kids really enjoy painting their best-loved friends from books. A nice idea is for Granny to write out a short extract from a favourite book, which the grandchild can then illustrate with their drawings. The resulting artwork could be framed and hung on the wall – in the child's bedroom or elsewhere.

A trip to the theatre – why not take your grandchild to see their favourite book live on stage? There are many touring productions for stories like *The Tiger Who Came to Tea* – the experience will be unforgettable.

> 'Our great grandparents: they spoil you rotten, feed you treats – and always have time for one last story.'
>
> SARAH BROWN

Fun days out

Grandchildren do not need to be bribed with expensive gifts and extravagant outings. There are so many inexpensive days out that can provide fun for children of all ages (and will be extremely interesting to their grandparents also).

By no means an exhaustive review, this section gives just a tiny taste of some possible treats to whet your appetite.

'Being grandparents sufficiently removes us from the responsibilities so that we can be friends.'

ALLAN FROME

∾ Get ready to research ∾

There are a variety of Internet sites you can look at for inspiration for days out with the grandkids. You can also find information in local visitor centres, hotels and B&Bs. Some destinations are only suitable when the weather is fine; others provide indoor fun as well.

It's always clever to research in advance as some of the venues are not open all year round, and some may be too far afield or too pricey. And there's nothing worse than a disappointed grandchild!

∾ Animal action ∾

Animals are a great delight to all ages, but especially for children who live in towns, who don't usually encounter anything other than domesticated animals.

There will be a natural instinct to 'reach out and touch' the animals – so remember to take some anti-bacterial wipes with you, and double check that children wash their hands after petting the creatures.

After that, your only dilemma will be which animal to see next!

Zoos

Zoos are endlessly fascinating whatever your age. The chance to see rare, exotic and endangered animals from all four corners of the globe just can't be beaten. Many zoos also offer informative keeper talks at feeding time.

There was an era when zoos were frowned upon by some, but many now do fantastic work with endangered species, and most go all out to ensure they provide a great day trip for all the family.

City farms

Farms are also full of fascination and fun, particularly for urban children – sometimes with unexpected results.

SLOBBER CITY

One little girl was taken to a rare breeds farm by her grandparents. They purchased a small bag of animal food for her, but she was too shy to offer it to the creatures on the farm.

Her granny, in an attempt to prove that the animals were tame enough to be hand-fed, took some food pellets from the bag and stuck out her hand in front of one of the cows. The result was pretty sloppy, and when the little girl was later collected by her dad, the first thing she said was, 'And the cow slobbered all over Granny!'

Many city farms house a great variety of farm animals to delight both young and old: pigs, donkeys, calves, sheep, small animals and feathered friends. They also offer a host of activities, from a pony ride to helping muck out the pigs – though some children (and grannies) might need to be persuaded to join in that one! – as well as quizzes, treasure trails and animal-spotting competitions.

Some working farms offer real 'hands-on' experiences, where you might find lambs or kids to bottle-feed, eggs to collect and pigs or cattle to feed. Plus you can take a goat or a ferret for a walk and handle young animals. There are activities both indoors and outside – so there's fun to be had, whatever the weather.

Wildlife and safari parks

If you're feeling a little more adventurous, you could try one of the wildlife parks dotted around the country. These contain many species that children have probably admired after seeing them on the telly or in films, but have likely never encountered face to face.

Usually set in beautiful landscaped parkland, there are some engrossing collections to see, including many very rare and endangered species. Birds, mammals, reptiles, invertebrates, creepy-crawlies, snakes, frogs, butterflies – you name it, there's somewhere you can go to see it and enjoy a great day out.

TIP

To avoid disappointment, make certain that your car is suitable for a safari-park outing: some vehicles, such as soft-tops, are restricted.

Aquariums

The world under the sea is full of fabulous creatures and you can see some of the weirdest, most enthralling and deadliest animals on the planet. There was a time when aquaria were rather dull leaky places in which murky tanks were filled with grey fish – some big, some not so big. Not any more!

Nowadays, aquaria teem with a plethora of colour-ful underwater life from faraway places, all housed in high-specification, bright, beautiful, fully interactive spaces designed specifically to care for the inhabitants and to educate and inform the visiting public.

✄ Museums ✄

Museums are no longer the fusty, boring places you might remember from your childhood. There are now many child- (and granny-!) friendly museums peppered all over the country, with quite a few of them boasting interactive displays.

You can find museums devoted to the most obscure and wonderful subjects, so while a visit to the Natural History Museum or the Science Museum is always great fun, why not try out some of the lesser known attractions, or investigate your area for museums devoted to local industries, dignitaries or events?

✆ Art galleries ✆

A good many art galleries will try to make your visit as child-friendly as possible by having story sessions, or making art materials available for children to play with while you are looking at the real thing. Take advantage of these when you can and give yourself a chance to really enjoy the day out too.

✆ Public transport ✆

Children have a great fascination for vehicles of all descriptions, and will often be delighted by a simple journey by bus or train.

For something really special, there are numerous steam railways throughout Britain that still go from A to B, making a day out a glorious adventure.

↜ **The circus** ↝

All children love the circus! There are still several touring circuses and you may be lucky enough to have one of them in your area when your grandchildren are visiting.

↜ **Nature walks** ↝

According to website www.grandparents.about.com, seven out of ten grandparents take their grandkids on walks, so it's really not true that today's children are only happy playing computer games.

Trees, flowers and other plants are interesting to look at and touch. Do tell little children not to put them in their mouths, but encourage them to make use of their other senses as they explore the natural world. Take trips to lakesides, forests, fields and riversides – the flora and fauna are simply captivating.

TIP

Never walk further than the child is capable of, otherwise – unless you've brought the pushchair along – you may find yourself carrying the child back to the car, or even all the way home.

Leaf rubbings

To add another dimension to your nature trail experience, why not combine it with this artistic activity?

YOU WILL NEED

- Fresh leaves
- White paper
- Crayons

METHOD

1. When out walking with the grandchildren, collect some interestingly shaped leaves in a plastic bag.

2. Once home, place a sheet of white paper on a flat surface and put a fresh leaf on top of it, vein side up. Lay another sheet of paper over the leaf in the position you want.

3. Peel the paper off a wax crayon and gently rub it on its side over the top sheet of paper. An image of the leaf will appear as if by magic!

4. Older children can write the name of the leaf (if you know it) on the sheet of paper.

'The simplest toy, one which even the youngest child can operate, is called a grandparent.'

SAM LEVENSON

I remember Granny

No one makes an impression in our lives like Granny does. She is the wonderwoman who can soothe any ill, make any game fun, bake delectable treats and give the warmest, most all-embracing hugs.

This section takes a look at the impact some grandmothers had on the world, and what their grandchildren recall about them.

> 'Elephants and grandchildren never forget.'
>
> ANDY ROONEY

✍ Jilly Cooper ❧

Author Jilly Cooper recently spoke about her mother's mother, Catherine Whincup, in the *Daily Mail*. Cooper said of her: 'A beauty even to the end, she had rose-petal skin, innocent blue eyes and swept-up white hair, with a rakish blonde streak at the front from chain-smoking.

'A clergyman's wife, she was intensely gentle, a great giggler and a chronic pessimist, who was teased and yet adored by all her grandchildren.'

✍ Agatha Christie ✍

According to recently discovered audiotapes found by her grandson, Mathew Prichard, novelist Agatha Christie modelled the famous character of Miss Marple on her own grandmother.

Christie dictated the tapes in the mid 1960s. They carry her description of Jane Marple – and reveal how she partially based the genteel sleuth on her grandma.

Though the author had always claimed that Miss Marple was in no way 'a picture of my grandmother', on the tapes she admitted that the two shared an important trait, as reported in the *Telegraph*:

Although a completely cheerful person, [my grandmother] always expected the worst of anyone and everything. And, with almost frightening accuracy, she was usually proved right.

'You do not really understand something unless you can explain it to your grandmother.'

ALBERT EINSTEIN

✍ Sarah Brown ✍

Writing in her book *Grandparents*, Sarah Brown, wife of PM Gordon Brown, commented: 'Most people who are lucky enough to have met their grandparents have wonderful childhood memories of them.

'My mum's mother was a gentle woman who had travelled the world with my grandfather in the diplomatic service. She spoke five languages, but what I remember most are her fried chicken bucket nights, which were the biggest treat imaginable for me and my brothers.

'We would gather a mountain of food and eat ourselves stupid while talking non-stop – all of us at the same time. Through it all, she would remain calm.'

✍ Caity Sue Treadwell ✍

One of the women interviewed for this book, Caity Sue recalled the following about her granny: 'My father's mother was this little Native American woman (Cherokee) with a long braid down her back. She was an amazingly strong woman; a widow who did not remarry until her children were grown.

'She bowed to no one and did what she had to do to raise her children. She took in laundry, cleaned houses – she worked hard and it showed in her face: she had lots of lines.

'When my father went into the military at eighteen, he would send his mother money every single month. She refused to spend it. Instead, she put it in the bank and when he came home on leave several years later, she gave him that money to buy a car.'

'Everyone needs to have access both to grandparents and grandchildren in order to be a full human being.'

MARGARET MEAD

The family tree

Inevitably the day will come when one of your grand-children asks, 'Where did I come from?'

It's probably best to leave the 'birds and the bees' explanation to their parents, but it might bring up another interesting subject – the family tree.

> 'Becoming a grandparent is worth waiting for. Grandparents are, or can be, the bedrock on which the rest of the family stands, adding stability and encompassing strong and lasting relationships across the generations. They're a kind of human cement which holds the family together.'
>
> DR MIRIAM STOPPARD

৩ **Where did I come from?** ৩

This is a tricky subject for children to grasp. It's difficult enough for adults to work out family relationships (for example, what is a second cousin or a cousin once removed?), but seemingly impossible for a small child even to imagine their parents and you as children.

When you mention that Mummy was once a little girl, *your* little girl, the child's first reaction is disbelief. Imagining you as a little girl who has (or had) a mummy is *beyond* disbelief!

৩ **Making a family tree** ৩

Making a family tree can be an interesting and heart-warming exercise, and will help your grandchildren to get their heads around the conundrum of family.

A family tree is a chart of information showing the relationships of family members, past and present. There are all sorts of blank templates you can download from the Internet for this purpose, but it's simple enough just to draw a diagram.

TIP

If you really get into it, you might find that you have to add many branches, so if you only want to do this once, it is best to start at the bottom and draw the branches as and when you come to them.

Information is everything

Before you actually make your chart, you must gather information.

Confused about how to begin? Start by recording what you already know about your family members. Begin with the child you are doing this with and work backwards.

TIP

You can store your information manually on record cards, in a notebook or on the computer.

What to record

You should record the following data for each person: name, date and place of birth, date and place of death, spouse (plus marriage date), children and parents.

If there are any other interesting facts about them, you can add those as well.

Family tree branches

- Begin with the child in question, plus siblings if any.

- The next layer is the child's parents and step-parents, and their further children if applicable.

- Then add your generation: you, your husband(s), other children and their children, and so forth.

🌷 The next tier is your parents and their siblings.

🌷 Then your grandparents and their siblings.

For relatives beyond your grandparents, you will likely need to consult secondary sources for data compilation.

✎ A helping hand ✐

Once the 'easy' entries are completed, you may need more help. So ask your relatives about other family members: this will save you time and effort before searching through official records.

'Surely, two of the most satisfying experiences in life must be those of being a grandchild or a grandparent.'

DONALD A. NORBERT

Helpful websites

When you have exhausted family assistance, there are various online sources where you can search for your ancestors. Look for your UK ancestors here:

www.ancestry.co.uk

www.GenesReunited.co.uk

www.findmypast.com/Family_Tree

If your forbears came from other countries, it is more complicated, but there are books and genealogy websites that can help you, for example:

> http://genealogy.about.com/od/europe/Europe.htm
> http://genealogy.about.com/od/asia/Genealogy_in_Asia_the_Pacific.htm

And if you have American or African ancestors, you could try these:

> http://www.olivetreegenealogy.com/usa/
> http://genealogy.about.com/od/africa/Africa.htm

What a wonderful way to get the entire family involved!

Grannies in the news

Grannies certainly get out and about! These granny-related stories hit the headlines. They make for fascinating reading ...

> 'What children need most are the essentials that grandparents provide in abundance. They give unconditional love, kindness, patience, humour, comfort, lessons in life. And, most importantly, cookies.'
>
> RUDOLPH GIULIANI

৶ Rent a granny ৶

Finding the time to do everything needed in life is always tough for parents, particularly working mums and dads. But in Berlin, Germany, there's an unusual solution for folks who need more time: the rent-a-granny service.

Roswita Winterstein came up with the idea in 1989, when many Communist kindergartens throughout the city were being shut down. With single-parent households on the rise and childcare difficult to find, the novel idea of renting a grandparent proved the answer to many mothers' prayers.

The service became so successful that it opened its second office in 2007.

At a loose end

Winterstein says that, after retirement, many of her friends began to realize that there was more to life than doing the housework or going on holiday, especially for those without their own grandchildren to dote on.

Service with a smile

Roswita's agency now employs 150 grandparents, mostly women, who are carefully screened and matched with younger families. Some rent-a-grannies like their work so much that they do it for free, building up a real relationship with the children they look after.

The word is spreading

Today, Berlin is not the only location blessed with grannies for hire. A new 'grannies-for-rent' service in Poland brings together elderly people without families, and people who miss having real grandparents.

While in Belgium ...

In July 2009, a new service launched that enabled people to drop off their grandparents at a foster family for a couple of hours, or even overnight.

It costs €2.50 an hour or €25 a night, and is only available in Flanders.

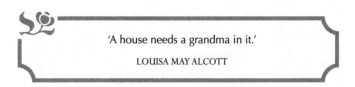

'A house needs a grandma in it.'

LOUISA MAY ALCOTT

๙ Hats on to grannies! ๛

A new bespoke beanie company has launched the UK's first brand knitted entirely by grandmas.

When the founder of Grannies Inc., Kate Mowat, was recruiting knitters for her new venture, she found that they were all of an older generation. So she decided to take advantage of their experience and turn it into a commercial feature.

Snow more reindeer jumpers

Customers get the advantage of years of knitting experience, and the grannies get to make some extra money. But perhaps best of all, because the women now have something different to knit, there will be less reindeer jumpers and knitted animals come Christmas time!

୶ Granny's new flatmate ୬

An American company, iRobot, has launched a new live-in helper for grannies that it hopes will eventually make grotty nursing homes a thing of the past.

The robotic assistant is strong enough to carry an adult up a steep flight of stairs, clever enough to dispense pills and monitor vital signs – and savvy enough to call for an ambulance in an emergency.

iRobot says it plans to give an extra 'one million years of independent living' to elderly people around the world through its innovative creation.

However, as *The Times* advises, just don't expect much from it in the way of conversation – or, perhaps more to the point, bingo skills.

'Grandchildren are God's way of compensating us for growing old.'

MARY H. WALDRIP

୶ Granny on eBay ୬

Senior surfers are commonplace these days, so this story was not some shock piece about a grandma doing a spot of Internet shopping – rather, it was about a granny up for sale!

Ten-year-old Zoe Pemberton put her sixty-one-year-old granny Marian Goodall on eBay in an attempt to cheer her up after Marian hurt her knee. Following eBay's rules for an honest appraisal of her goods, Zoe described Marian as someone who could be 'annoying' by 'moaning a lot', but commended her for being 'very cuddly'.

The story hit the national headlines after bids for Marian reached £20,000. Marian's son, Thomas Pemberton, commented to the *Daily Mail*: 'I was amazed, but my mum wasn't. She said she was worth millions.' Good old Gran!

Making gifts with Granny

Everyone appreciates a personal gift – one that has been made with love, especially for them.

A lovely idea is to conspire with your grandchild to make gifts for all the family. Such creative presents should be in line with the child's abilities, even if they need a little help from you.

'An hour with your grandchildren can make you feel young again. Anything longer than that and you start to age quickly.'

GENE PERRET

✑ Let inspiration strike ✑

There are countless homemade gift ideas that children will delight in creating. Here are just a few suggestions to get you started:

- Pictures that children draw can be turned into all sorts of wonderful presents – think calendars, place mats and T-shirts, to name a few.

- Old greetings cards can be cut up and used for collages – the children can then add to these by drawing or painting on extra bits.

- There is always the painted rock, which Mum or Dad can use as a paperweight.

- Another idea is jewellery. Teaching a child to string beads together is a lovely way to spend an afternoon, and boys seem to like this just as much as girls.

❧ The grandmother necklace ❧

Although this gift is called a grandmother necklace, it can be made for any member of the family. The basic idea is to make a kind of charm necklace – or bracelet – where each charm represents a child or family member.

So, for example, you could make one for an auntie – each charm would represent her various nieces and nephews; or for a mother (charms represent her children); or even for a child (charms could represent their siblings).

Charmed, I'm sure

So, how do you make a grandmother necklace?

1. Firstly, decide how you want to portray the family members. What sort of charms do you want to use? Here are some ideas:

    ■ Heads and shoulders modelled from clay or FIMO, painted with the facial features of each person, and perhaps even labelled with their names.

TIP

If you choose this option, remember to ensure you have made provision for attaching the charms to the necklace, e.g. by adding a metal loop.

    ■ Symbols depicting the people, such as little cars for the boys and mini teddies for the girls, both of which items you'll find ready-made in craft shops (along with many other ideas, e.g. ladybirds, trains, frogs, dolls, butterflies, etc.).

    ■ Painted wooden face beads, on which you can write the names of the people.

2.   Once the charms are decided upon, you might choose to space out the symbolic family members with hearts or other beads.

3.   After you've finalized your design, use a leather thong or nylon wire for the necklace.

TIP

Leather has the advantage of being more versatile than nylon: the necklace owner will be able to tie the thong to different lengths depending on what they are wearing.

---

4.   Thread the beads and charms along the length of the wire or thong, then tie the two ends together securely. Voilà!

TIP

If the family is joined by a new baby at some point in the future – and needs to be represented on the necklace – remember to add another charm to the necklace then.

✒ **Fabulous fudge** ✒

This is a wonderful Christmas gift and an easy confection to make with your grandchildren for them and their parents. If any of your family has a nut allergy, simply omit the nuts.

Makes 81 squares

INGREDIENTS

> 500g (18oz) plain *or* milk chocolate chips
> 6 tbsp golden syrup
> 85g (3oz) sifted icing sugar
> 6 tbsp evaporated milk
> 1 tsp vanilla essence
> 55–115g (2–4oz) chopped walnuts or pecans (optional)
> 170g (6oz) dried cranberries (optional, but delicious)

METHOD

1. In a heavy saucepan over a low heat, melt the chocolate chips with the golden syrup. Remove from the heat.

2. Add the icing sugar, evaporated milk and vanilla essence. Stir vigorously until the mixture is thick and glossy.

3. If using, add the nuts and cranberries now, mixing together well.

4. Spread the mixture evenly into a clingfilm- or foil-lined 20cm (8-inch) square pan. Cover and chill until firm (roughly 2-3 hours).

5. Turn the fudge out of the pan onto a cutting
    board and cut into 2.5cm (1-inch) squares. Store,
    covered, in the refrigerator.

Added extras

The great thing about this simple fudge recipe is that it's
easy to play around with according to personal taste. Here
are some easy additions or substitutions if you fancy fooling
around with fudge:

- You can substitute chopped dried cherries for the
  cranberries.

- Add one tablespoon of instant coffee granules *or*
  espresso when you are melting the chocolate.

- Use white chocolate chips instead of the plain or milk
  chocolate.

- Use unsalted pistachio nuts instead of walnuts or
  pecans.

- Add one tablespoon of grated orange rind *or*
  crystallized ginger to the mixture just before you pour
  it into the tin to solidify.

- Add one teaspoon of ground cinnamon *or* cardamom at
  the same stage.

⁓ Toasted almond truffles ⁓

Creamy and rich, these lovely chocolate confections are a breeze to make and a delight to receive.

Makes 24 truffles

INGREDIENTS

> 120ml (4fl oz) evaporated milk
>
> 4 tbsp caster sugar
>
> 340g (12oz) milk chocolate chips
>
> ½ tsp vanilla essence
>
> ½ tsp almond essence (optional)
>
> 115g (4oz) flaked almonds, toasted and chopped

METHOD

1. In a small saucepan, combine the evaporated milk and sugar. Bring to the boil over a medium-low heat and then boil, stirring constantly, for three minutes. Remove from the heat.

2. Mix in the chocolate chips and stir vigorously until the mixture is smooth. Stir in the vanilla and almond essences if using.

3. Refrigerate the mixture for about two hours.

4. On a work surface covered with greaseproof paper, roll the mixture into 24 2.5cm (1-inch) balls. Spread out the almonds on the paper and roll the chocolate balls in the nuts.

5. Put into a lidded plastic container and refrigerate until ready to eat or give as a gift.

In Granny's footsteps

Sometimes the start in life that grannies give their grandchildren, or the example they set through their passions and pursuits, inspires those kids so much that they follow in their grandmothers' footsteps.

That can be intentional or accidental – but it happens more often than you might think!

'To my grandchildren, Maiya, Atticus and O'sha, in the knowledge that they'll end up like their parents and grandparents … ballsy, truth-telling, free-thinking, heart-bleeding, myth-debunking, non-conforming and hell-raising activists.'

ANITA RODDICK, IN THE INSCRIPTION AT THE
START OF HER BOOK *BUSINESS AS UNUSUAL*

✍ An inspiration ✍

Grannies are a very special kind of adult in a child's life. Long associated with love, they are also an inspiration in the way they live their lives.

The phrase 'like grandmother, like grandchild' could be applied to the following examples …

Sylvia and Helen Pankhurst

Sylvia Pankhurst was a notable campaigner for the suffragette movement in the UK, and a lifelong advocate for women's rights. In 1956, she moved to Ethiopia, where she fought to improve conditions for mothers and babies; when she died there, in 1960, she was given a full state funeral at which she was named an 'honorary Ethiopian'.

Sylvia's granddaughter, Helen, now works for WaterAid in Ethiopia. She too is involved in the fight to improve women's lives.

In 1984, Dr Pankhurst, speaking in London, said, 'Women need to remember that it was only two generations ago when women didn't have the vote. All women should vote and remember the indignity and abuse that their grandmothers went through.'

If Sylvia were alive today, she would be proud.

Toshiko D'Elia and Ben Diestel

Toshiko D'Elia is a world-record holder and the first woman aged over fifty to run a marathon in less than three hours. She's also become something of a mentor to her eighteen-year-old grandson, Ben Diestel, who has literally followed in her footsteps by taking up running.

Though still a junior in high school, Ben has a personal best of 16:04 for the cross-country 5K and his future looks bright.

Whenever he wins a race, he and his gran go out for sushi together to celebrate.

> '[My grandmother] has been very inspiring. I think she has done a fantastic job and I look up to what she does.'
>
> PRINCE WILLIAM

Alice Keppel and Camilla, Duchess of Cornwall

Alice Keppel was the most famous mistress of King Edward VII – and the great-grandmother of Camilla, Duchess of Cornwall. Camilla, of course, was the mistress of Prince Charles for thirty-odd years, before their marriage on 9 April 2005.

Sadly, Camilla never knew her great-grandmother as she was just a tiny baby when Alice died.

Christine and Annabelle Bond

In 1929, at the age of twenty-one, mountaineering pioneer Christine Bond became one of the first Western women to climb in the Himalayas when she embarked on an expedition with legendary mountaineer Hugh Rutledge, charting previously unmapped parts of Nepal.

Seventy-six years later, her granddaughter Annabelle Bond completed the arduous Seven Summits challenge – reaching the highest peak on each of the seven continents – and did so in just 360 days, making her the fastest woman climber in the world, and one of only 115 people to have achieved this remarkable feat.

Midway through her granddaughter's undertaking, Christine commented to the *Independent*: 'I think Annabelle got the infection from me. We can't resist things like this.'

Many happy returns

Birthdays in a young child's life are just about the most exciting thing to happen all year. As a grandmother, you'll love the opportunity to celebrate them too.

With each birthday that passes, the child grows older. This brings a whole new level to your relationship, and their increasing maturity means the bond between you will deepen even further.

Children are also fascinated by your birthday – if only in part because they can't believe how *old* Granny is!

'My grandchildren think I'm the oldest person in the world. And after two or three hours with them, I believe it also.'

GENE PERRET

๑๑ **Birthday call** ๑๑

A young boy rang to wish his granny a happy birthday and asked how old she was. The lady replied, 'Sixty-two.'

There was silence for a minute, then the boy asked: 'Did you start at one?'

๑๑ **Giving gifts** ๑๑

If you are unsure about what presents to give your grandchildren for their birthdays, or other celebrations, it might interest you to know that the toys grandparents played with as children are making a comeback.

The children may have all sorts of fancy electronic fads on their wish lists, but give them old-style toys and not only will they be provided with hours of fun, but your bank balance will look a little healthier too.

Old-fashioned toys

The fact is that today's children still love to play with yesterday's toys. One of the pluses of this is that both children and their grandparents know how to play with them!

Here are a few suggestions of gifts you might like to give:

 Marbles (perhaps with a marble run)

 A cup and ball

 A skipping rope

🌷 A teddy bear

🌷 A building set such as Meccano

Doll's houses and rocking horses are still beloved too. They can be very expensive, but not when you consider that they are often passed from generation to generation.

Something special

A birthday can be an opportunity to give something very special to a child – perhaps something personalized, or even something that might become a family heirloom in the years to come. How about one of these suggestions?

🌷 Silver spoon

🌷 Charm bracelet

🌷 Jewellery box

🌷 Framed artwork from a children's book

🌷 Engraved silver mug

And now for something completely different

When a three-year-old boy opened his birthday gift from his grandmother, he discovered a water pistol. He squealed with delight and headed for the nearest sink, turning on the taps full blast.

His mother was not so pleased. She turned to Granny and said, 'I'm surprised at you. Don't you remember how we used to drive you crazy with water guns?'

Granny smiled and then replied, 'I remember.'

๛ Granny's birthday ๑

Because birthdays loom so large in a child's calendar, they are always thrilled when it's Granny's birthday too. Let them share in your big day:

- Request that they lead the singing of 'Happy Birthday'.

- Commission a family portrait for an extra-special birthday – it will be something you'll truly treasure.

- Teach them 'When I'm Sixty-Four' by The Beatles and have a sing-along.

- Ask for their help in blowing all your candles out!

๛ Age is relative ๑

A little girl asked her grandmother how old she was. Grandma coyly replied, 'Well, I'm not exactly sure.'

Her granddaughter advised her to look in her underwear: 'Mine says I'm four to six.'

Grandma's wisdom

Everybody knows that grannies are the wisest creatures on earth. Grandmothers have become the go-to women when advice is needed or a helping hand is called for.

Their knowledge and zest should never be underestimated.

> 'Becoming a grandmother is wonderful. One moment you're just a mother. The next you are all-wise and prehistoric.'
>
> PAM BROWN

❧ Eat your pound of dirt ❧

Children are so over-sanitized these days that they seem to catch colds and sniffles at the drop of a hat. But Granny believed in toughening children up. She said you have to 'eat your pound of dirt before you die'.

Recent study

And Granny was right. According to Californian scientists, getting dirty as a child may well be the answer to a healthier, allergy-free life.

Too clean?

Researchers found that being too clean could impair the body's capacity to heal itself and prevent allergies. Helpful bacteria that live on the skin normally leap into action for us, but today's very sanitized environments – full of antibacterial hand washes and so on – are jeopardizing this natural process.

Worrying result

More and more children in developed countries are becoming prone to allergies such as hayfever and eczema as a result.

❧ Nit-picking ❧

Nits are a natural part of every grandmother's life – it's more than likely your grandchildren will suffer from these pesky creatures' attention during their childhood.

The itching and subsequent shampooing is never fun, but Granny can help by making a game out of the whole process.

One grandmother, Renée Faure, did just that when she wrote this silly poem to amuse her grandsons.

A louse in the house

There's a louse in the house!
Not a mouse? No, a louse!
'How do you know?' she said.
'I've been itching and scratching my head
All day, and in bed, till it's red!' they both said.

'Oh my dear, I do fear, bad times are here …
And it's not at all nice!' She uttered it twice.
She was worried, then hurried and scurried
To find what device would suffice to get rid of the lice.

She shampooed and lathered their heads with foam
Ten minutes they sat with foam on each dome
Not a moan or groan because it was known
At the end every louse would be dead – quite alone.

↶ Council of grandmothers ↷

In 2004, a spiritual teacher named Jyoti organized a gathering of thirteen indigenous grandmothers from all around the globe. She wanted to call them together to pool their ancient knowledge.

(It is said that she and the grandmothers had had a vision that such a sharing of experience was needed for the survival of the next generations.)

From three different continents, different countries and completely different cultures and traditions, these grandmothers were brought together to bring hope and healing to the world and the future.

Legacy

Today, the council of grandmothers still meets: to share knowledge and advice, to run workshops and sessions, and to support worthy projects and causes.

A documentary film, *For the Next Seven Generations*, has been made about the group.

Making your own fun

P art of the joy of being a grandmother is that, for the most part, you get to do fun things with your grandchildren and leave all the responsibilities to their parents. You've raised your children; now it's their turn to raise theirs. This allows you to enjoy the children in a way that isn't possible when you are the mother.

'Grandparents are similar to a piece of string –
handy to have around and easily wrapped around the
fingers of their grandchildren.'

AUTHOR UNKNOWN

✑ Good fun = gratis ✑

Good fun does not have to cost a lot of money. There are many projects you can undertake with your grand-kids that are free.

You might need to buy some materials, such as paper, card and paints, but you can also make use of items you have around the house, such as dried pasta, string, yarn, ribbons or shoeboxes.

Doing things together will make the bond between you and your grandchildren even stronger.

❧ Doll's house ❧

You can have a lot of fun constructing and decorating this doll's house with a small grandchild.

YOU WILL NEED

- Several shoeboxes
- Pencil
- Scissors
- Wrapping paper
- Glue or double-sided Sellotape
- Carpet remnants
- Miniature furniture and people
- Paints and brushes
- Two shoebox lids (optional – for roof)
- Cardboard loo roll (optional – for chimney)
- Sheet of cardboard (optional – for en-suite bathroom partitions!)

METHOD

1. Firstly, you have to decide how many rooms you want to have in the house. You will need one shoebox per room and they should all be the same size box.

TIP

A modest house would have a sitting room, a kitchen/dining room and two bedrooms. NB: an area of each bedroom could be partitioned with card-board for en-suite bathrooms, if desired.

---

2. Along the length of one side of each shoebox you're using, draw and cut out squares for windows. Don't forget to draw the front door on one box!

3. Stick bits of wrapping paper on the 'walls' for wallpaper and place remnants of carpet on the floors for 'rugs'. Furniture and people can either be purchased or made (if you're feeling particularly crafty): add these to the rooms now.

4. Once the rooms are decorated, put the boxes in the order in which you want to place the rooms and fasten them together with glue or tape.

5. If having a roof, place two of the box tops in a 'V' shape over the house. Balance them together and secure with tape. If desired, you can even make a chimney out of a cardboard loo roll! Cut a suitably sized circle halfway

up one of the box tops, then ease the loo roll inside the hole.

6. When the house is fully assembled, you can paint its exterior with an opaque paint or painstakingly draw bricks on the sides. Some craft shops sell 'brick' wrapping paper, which also does the job!

7. Have hours of fun playing.

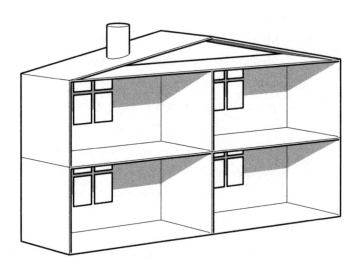

ᥥ **Rock-star guitar** ᥦ

This is an easy and satisfying project, perfect for young grandkids with a passion for music.

YOU WILL NEED

- One shoebox (with lid)
- One empty kitchen towel cardboard roll
- Scissors
- Sellotape
- Four or five elastic bands of various lengths and widths
- Paints and brushes

METHOD

1. Take the shoebox and cut a small hole, the size of the diameter of the kitchen towel cardboard roll, in one of its shorter sides.
2. Insert the cardboard roll in the hole and tape it into place. This will be the handle of the guitar.
3. Take the shoebox lid and cut a round hole in the centre. Place the lid back on the box.
4. Take the elastic bands and stretch them length-ways over the hole in the lid, fastening them securely.
5. Paint your guitar as decoratively as you wish.
6. When the paint is dry, try plucking the 'strings' (elastic bands). You will hear some semblance of music!

ೞ **Sock puppet** ೞ

YOU WILL NEED

- A bunch of stray socks (any colour or pattern)
- Scissors
- Card
- Coloured felt remnants
- Glue
- Needle and thread
- Buttons
- Yarn/wool

METHOD

1. For each puppet you are going to make, put the sock over your left hand (if you are right-handed) with your fingers and thumb in the toe of the sock.
2. Spread your thumb and fingers apart and cut a slit in the sock in the space between your thumb and fingers.
3. Cut an oval shape out of the card about 7.5cm (3 inches) wide × 12.5cm (5 inches) long and cut an identical shape from a piece of felt. This will be the puppet's mouth.
4. Glue the felt to the card and then fold in half vertically.
5. Sew the folded card to the sock so that the felt is visible (i.e. affix it where the base of your fingers are once your hand is inside the sock, so as you open and close your fingers and thumb, the mouth 'speaks').

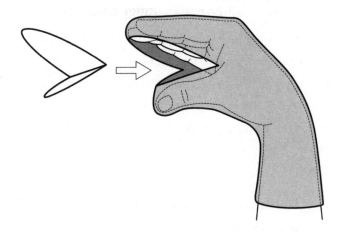

6. Make eyes from buttons (they don't have to match) and hair from the yarn, sewing them onto the sock. Spots and stripes made out of felt can also be fixed to the 'body' of the puppet with either glue or thread.

TIP

Involve your grandchildren by asking them to choose the colours and shapes of the puppet's features, and which buttons are used for the eyes. Question them about the personality of the puppet: for example, do red buttons for eyes make this a 'baddie' puppet?

When you have a few sock puppet characters, you can write a script and put on a puppet show.

✺ **Papier-mâché piggy bank** ✺

This is a rather more complex project – and a messy one! But for those willing to take on the challenge of mixing up the papier-mâché paste, and who have the patience and/or time to wait out the two days it will take for the piggy bank to dry, it's a very lovely task to undertake.

YOU WILL NEED

- Papier-mâché paste (see below)
- Newspaper
- A round balloon
- Empty egg box
- Masking tape
- Cardboard
- Pipe cleaner
- Scissors
- Pin
- Paints and brushes
- Varnish or Mod Podge (a glue and sealer obtained from craft shops)

METHOD

1. Put aprons on the children and yourself.
2. Make the paste. Put 1.4 litres (2½ pints) of water in a large saucepan with 340g (12oz) of flour and 2 tbsp of salt. Heat until the mixture has the consistency of double cream. Remove from the heat and cool.

3. Tear the newspaper into strips.

4. Blow up the balloon and tie a knot at the end. This will be the pig's body.

5. Make the snout. Tape one cup from the egg box onto the knotted end of the balloon.

6. Cut two 'ears' from the cardboard and tape onto the balloon.

7. Make the legs: cut two circles from the cardboard and cut them in half. Form four cones and attach with tape to the underside of the pig.

8. Cut and form the pipe cleaner into a curly tail and tape onto the balloon's 'bottom'.

9. Paste four layers of newspaper strips over the pig and allow to dry for two days.

10. Cut a coin slit into the top of the pig and then burst the balloon with a pin.

11. Decorate with paint – not forgetting the pig's eyes and nostrils – and allow to dry.

12. Apply at least one coat of varnish or Mod Podge to the pig.

True tales

Being a granny is a rich source of humour and sweetness. There's nothing like stories from the front line of grandmotherhood. Here are a few choice ones, collected together for your enjoyment.

Bet you have your own tales to tell too!

'Being pretty on the inside means you don't hit your brother and you eat all your peas – that's what my grandma taught me.'

LORD CHESTERFIELD

ᨆ Back to the future ᨆ

One soon-to-be grandma's son was stationed in Okinawa, Japan. When he called her at work with the news of the child's birth, Granny was elated. She took down all the statistics and turned to relate them to her colleagues.

'I'm a grandmother!' she declared. 'It's a baby girl, and she weighs five pounds.'

'When was she born?' someone asked.

Recalling the date her son had told her, Granny paused, looked at the calendar, and then said in amazement, 'Tomorrow!'

✺ Skills ✺

Emma's granddaughter came to spend a few weeks with her. During the visit, Emma decided to teach her how to sew.

After she had gone through a lengthy explanation of how to thread the machine, her granddaughter stepped back, put her hands on her hips, and said in disbelief, 'You mean you can do *all* that, but you can't play my Game Boy?'

✺ Just nutty ✺

Little Johnny went to visit his grandma. She had a bowl of peanuts on the coffee table and Johnny asked if he could have some. They were really good, so he ate them all.

When he was leaving, he thanked his grandmother for the nuts. She responded, 'You're welcome, sweet-heart. Ever since I misplaced my dentures, all I can do is suck the chocolate off them.'

✑ Freckles ✐

An elderly woman and her granddaughter spent the day at the zoo. Lots of the children were getting their faces painted and the little girl joined the queue. The boy standing in front of her turned around and commented loudly, 'You've got so many freckles, there's no place to paint!'

Embarrassed, the girl dropped her head. Her grandmother knelt down next to her. 'I love your freckles. When I was a little girl, I always wanted freckles,' she said. 'Freckles are beautiful.'

The girl looked up. 'Really?'

'Of course,' said the grandmother. 'Why, just name me one thing that's prettier than freckles.'

The little girl thought for a moment, peered intensely into her grandma's face, and then softly whispered, 'Wrinkles.'

✑ Home at the airport ✐

A six-year-old was talking to some grown-ups about his granny's visit.

'Where does your granny live?' one of them asked.

'At the airport,' was the reply.

'The airport? Are you sure?'

'Yes,' said the child, 'when we want to see her, we go to pick her up at the airport. And when the visit's over, we just take her back there.'

✎ **Colours** ✎

A grandmother wanted to see how well her little grandson knew the names of colours, so she would point something out to him and ask if he knew what it was. Invariably, the answer was right.

Finally, after being asked many times, the boy said, 'Granny, shouldn't you know your colours by now?'

'One of life's greatest mysteries is how the boy who wasn't good enough to marry your daughter can be the father of the smartest grandchild in the world.'

JEWISH PROVERB

✎ **I swear** ✎

The children were sitting at the dinner table at Christmas. Helen's little grandson didn't appear to be eating his Brussels sprouts. So she asked him, 'Don't you like Brussels sprouts?'

'No,' Jack replied.

'Why?' she asked.

'Because they're buglocks,' he answered.

This didn't make any sense to the adults until they figured it out. Jack had heard one of the grown-ups swearing, melded the two words together in his head and concluded that this described something *disgusting*.

Now, whenever anyone in the family wants to swear, they say 'buglocks' instead.

> The moral of this story is that you should never say anything in front of children that you don't want repeated. Little pitchers have big ears, as my granny used to say …

✺ Faux pas ✺

Little Charlie and his family were having Sunday dinner at his grandmother's house. When Charlie received his plate, he started eating right away.

'Charlie! Please wait until we say our prayer,' said his mother.

'I don't need to,' the boy replied.

'Of course you do,' his mother insisted. 'We always say a prayer before eating at our house.'

'But that's at our house,' Charlie reasoned. 'This is Grandma's house and she *knows* how to cook!'

'Never have children, only grandchildren.'

GORE VIDAL

Acknowledgements

There are so many people to thank for making this book possible. First and foremost, Louise Dixon, editorial director at Michael O'Mara Books; my wonderful editor, Kate Moore, who pulled it all together beautifully; and the grannies on both sides of the pond and further afield whose brains I picked: Susan, Gillian, Renée, Carolyne, Sylvia, Pat T, Pat Z, Jennifer, Elaine, Kathryn, Caity Sue and Ann. Plus my wonderful husband, John, who always helps me enormously in my research and listens to all my thoughts.

Special thanks to Renée Faure for her permission to reproduce her poem 'A louse in the house' on page 143, and to Sandra L. Doty for her words on grandmothers on page 11.

Lee Faber